TRICIA GUILD ON COLOR

DECORATION · FURNISHING · DISPLAY

SPECIAL PHOTOGRAPHY BY DAVID MONTGOMERY

TEXT BY TRICIA GUILD WITH ELIZABETH WILHIDE

RIZZOLI
NEW YORK

For L.G. and R.P. . . . and his yellow

AUTHOR'S ACKNOWLEDGEMENTS
I would like to thank the following people who have contributed to this book:

David Montgomery for the quality of his light, Jeremy Hilder for helping him;
Jo Willer for her keen eye, constant support and encouragement;
Simon Jeffreys, Virginia Bruce, Lisa Guild, Nim Thompson and the team at Designers Guild;
Evelyn Shearer; from Conran Octopus Anne Furniss, Jo Bradshaw, Liz Wilhide, Jessica Walton,
Julia Golding and Meryl Lloyd for her patience and brilliant art direction.

Project Editor JOANNA BRADSHAW

Art Editor MERYL LLOYD

Picture Research JESSICA WALTON

Production JULIA GOLDING

First published in the United States of America in 1993 by
Rizzoli International Publications, Inc.,
300 Park Avenue South, New York, NY 10010

Originally published in Great Britain in 1992 by
Conran Octopus Limited

First paperback edition
published in 1995

Reprinted 1996, 1997

Paperback ISBN 0-8478-1877-2

Library of Congress Catalog Card Number: 92-61196

For details of Designers Guild fabrics featured in this book, please refer to the Fabric Directory on page 186.

Typeset by Hunters Armley Ltd.
Printed and bound in Hong Kong

CONTENTS

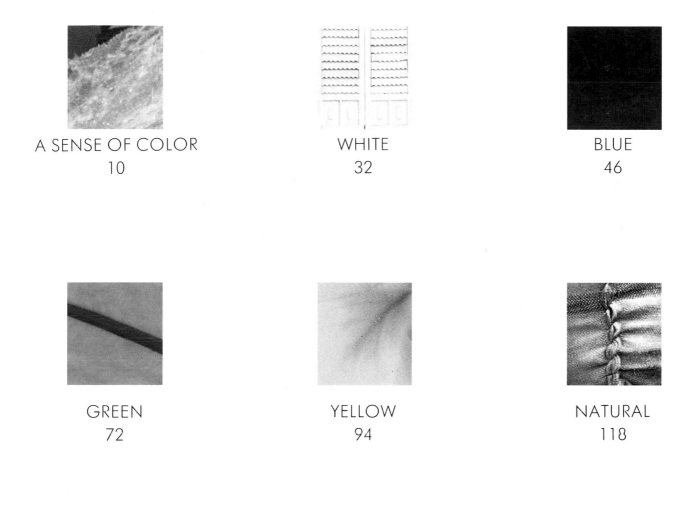

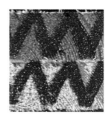

FOREWORD

"WHEN I CHOOSE A COLOR IT IS NOT BECAUSE OF ANY
SCIENTIFIC THEORY. IT COMES FROM OBSERVATION,
FROM FEELING, FROM THE INNERMOST NATURE OF
THE EXPERIENCE IN QUESTION".

HENRI MATISSE

My life and work have been deeply influenced by color
and its potential. This book is a celebration, a way of sharing
my involvement with color and the way it enhances
and enriches so many aspects of life.
It is the ultimate expression of vitality.

Tricia Guild

A SENSE OF COLOR

"SPRING IS TENDER, GREEN YOUNG CORN AND PINK
APPLE BLOSSOMS.
FALL IS THE CONTRAST OF THE YELLOW LEAVES AGAINST
VIOLET TONES.
WINTER IS THE SNOW WITH BLACK SILHOUETTES.
BUT NOW, IF SUMMER IS THE OPPOSITION OF BLUES
AGAINST AN ELEMENT OF ORANGE, IN THE GOLD BRONZE
OF THE CORN, ONE COULD PAINT A PICTURE WHICH
EXPRESSED THE MOOD OF THE SEASONS IN EACH OF THE
CONTRASTS OF THE COMPLEMENTARY COLORS . . ."

LETTER TO HIS BROTHER THEO,

VINCENT VAN GOGH

LIVING WITH COLOR

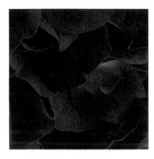

COLOR HAS THE POWER TO TRANSFORM THE SMALLEST OF SPACES INTO A VITAL AND UPLIFTING ENVIRONMENT.

We are fortunate to be living at a time when color is available to everyone. Color printing, color photography, color television are all relatively recent developments, and through these technological advances we are able now to acquire an entire visual education without even leaving the living room. Such constant exposure to colorful imagery was simply not available, even two generations ago.

In decoration, too, colors of every conceivable hue are achievable and affordable – in wallpaper, paint, fabric, carpet, and ceramic tile, so it has become easier than ever before to use color and to "live" color. An extraordinarily powerful subject and a fascinating tool, color can alter a domestic environment, enhancing the mood of an interior and improving the quality of life within.

Despite this new accessibility, many people are still remarkably hesitant when it comes to applying color in their own homes. There is a tendency to cling to stale color schemes which offer safe solutions and to opt for muddy non-colors rather than positive tones.

One reason for this hesitancy may be the dominance of the plain white wall in contemporary decoration, a legacy of "modern" movements in interior design and architecture resulting in a minimalism which has only recently been challenged. Another reason for present-day reticence in the use of color could well be that the instinctive handling of vivid color and rich pattern, skills which our ancestors enjoyed in previous centuries, has been lost. Despite a really rather limited choice of colors, both colonial and Victorian rooms were often surprisingly expressive and exuberant, proving that color can be uniquely uplifting, lending energy and life to an interior.

Perhaps the sheer breadth of choice available today is confusing, not to say intimidating. Easy, coordinated lines of fabric and paint help the nervous decorator assemble a coherent scheme, but this is at the cost of a great deal of vitality and creativity. Some people imagine that color is tiring to live with,

LIVING WITH COLOR

forgetting how dreary it is to sit in dull rooms without a spark of interest to stimulate the eye. Others think that color is only appropriate in hot places, where the light is strong. But cheerfulness is not the sole preserve of the sunny South: we only have to look at Scandinavian folk art and decoration to see how strong vivid greens and tomato reds are widely used to banish the misery of long, gray winter days.

Color has a profound impact on all our lives; its ability to transform surroundings, to excite a variety of reactions, to uplift and inspire is second to none. Our responses to it lie deep, almost defying analysis or explanation.

Color speaks directly, with an appeal that is almost visceral. It can influence powerfully by association, thru common uses embedded in culture, or by calling up personal experiences locked in the memory. Since civilization began, color has been one of the principal ways in which we express our creativity and *joie de vivre.* No matter how dormant or under-used, color sense can be brought back to life and encouraged to blossom. It starts with observation. Few people are born with an instinctive sense of color; more often than not, it has to be learned like any other skill. The eye is an incredibly sensitive organ which is capable of making millions of subtle color distinctions, so to ignore this potential depth of response would be like eating the same food every day.

One way of becoming acquainted with color is to build up a scrapbook of favorite color swatches, scraps of fabric, ribbon, postcards, photographs – anything that inspires you. Many people find they are attracted naturally to a certain family of colors – rich earth colors, or a variety of blues, for example. Others are drawn exclusively to a particular shade for a time, until a new color takes their fancy. Some women can become sensitized to a specific color during pregnancy, just as others have cravings for certain foods. This phenomenon appears in Nicholson Baker's novel *Room Temperature,* where the narrator describes his wife's obsession with cranberry red.

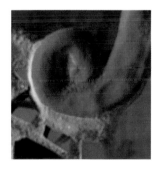

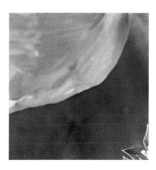

Color is so much a part of our lives and even our way of thinking that many people (myself included) unconsciously assign different colors to letters, numbers, or even sounds. For example, I have, since early childhood, experienced days of the week as particular colors: Monday is pale blue; Thursday is lime green. Friday is brown; Sunday is pink.

"Colors are the mother tongue of the subconscious," said Jung, and it is obvious from the central role that color has played in folklore and religions over many centuries, as well as its innumerable everyday associations, that color operates on many levels. Nearly every color at one time or in one culture or another has had spiritual connotations: color is literally magic. On a more prosaic level, the vast sums of money spent by advertising agencies in deciding which color will appeal most to the consumer testify to the powerful way in which color communicates values and feelings. Colors often remind people of something else sometimes from way back in their past.

From appreciating colors in all their richness and diversity, it is a short step to the endlessly fascinating exploration of color combinations. The electric mixtures, where the colors sing, the compatible families, where each color supports the others, and the simple graphic contrasts, all have an important role to play in decoration.

Color is subjective. But despite the individual nature of our reactions and responses, it is important to look at how color works – in theory and in practice, in nature, art and in science – before considering ways of using it successfully in our own surroundings.

THE NATURE OF COLOR

THE FRESH NEW GREEN OF BALINESE PADDY FIELDS SHOWS HOW NATURE CAN PROVIDE THE MOST BRILLIANT COLOR OF ALL.

The names people use to describe different colors can be very revealing. Leaf green, fuchsia, buttercup yellow, midnight blue, rose, nut brown, all conjure up the world of nature. It is not surprising that nature is one of the most rewarding sources of inspiration for those looking to extend their color vocabulary. Color begins with nature. And nature is what all our subjective color memories and responses ultimately have in common. Green is calming and restful because it is reminiscent of green fields, fresh new growth, and the landscape. Blue is expansive, airy, and watery like the sky and the sea. Yellow is warming and positive like the golden sun. Red is nature's accent – a danger signal, as in bright poisonous berries or deadly fungi, or the eye-catching attraction of a rooster's comb or display of feathers. The colors of childhood places, of gardens and flowers, are impressions that very often stay with us forever.

Sometimes nature close at hand is just too familiar to stimulate the imagination, which is why travel can be so reviving. The experience of seeing new landscapes under different conditions of light can change our whole perception of color. And after time away, we often see the colors in our own landscapes with fresh eyes. Seasonal change can provide much the same refreshing contrast.

Nature is not only a source of color ideas, it can also provide the colors themselves in the form of natural dyes and pigments. The oldest colors of all come from the earth, such as ocher and umber from clay, while colors obtained from animals and vegetables include madder, indigo, and cochineal (from crushed beetles). The art of using natural dyes was almost obliterated by the Industrial Revolution, but William Morris revived the technique when he experimented and perfected the use of natural colors in his printed fabrics. Compare a Morris pattern using natural dyes with a nineteenth-century equivalent created with the harsh chemical dyes of the period, and the difference in subtlety and color balance is obvious.

THE ART OF COLOR

While the color names we owe to nature may be beautifully evocative, for sheer precision it is hard to beat descriptions such as crimson, viridian, vermilion, burnt sienna, ultramarine, and cerulean blue. The terminology associated with artists' colors is rich and exact, making fine distinctions between different shades. We even see some colors through an artist's eyes. Titian red, for example, is a descriptive term that has passed into everyday usage as a result of the strikingly original tints achieved by this Italian Renaissance painter.

Nowhere has color been studied more intensely, its characteristics and potential explored more thoroughly, than in the work of artists – from Piero della Francesca, Bellini, and Vermeer to Monet, Van Gogh, Matisse, and Kandinsky. All artists necessarily have been concerned with color; some have been obsessed by it. Powerful insights into the use of color and the feelings and moods it can inspire can be found in a wide variety of artists' work: the jewel-like intensity of medieval paintings, where color has its own iconography; the delicate fresco colors of a Giotto or a Botticelli, the luminous tonalities of Piero della Francesca, as well as Titian, Vermeer, and, of course, Turner, with his elemental vision of light and color.

Closer to our time, particularly after the scientific nature of color began to be understood, color itself became the subject rather than an aspect of composition or an adjunct of naturalism. The paintings of the Impressionists show a passionate desire to record what the artist really saw at a particular moment, to be true to perception. In this they were responding directly to nineteenth-century advances in optics. Light was broken up into bright patches, dots, flecks, and brushstrokes of color, a fluid and sometimes dazzling palette which vibrated on the eye. Monet's series of paintings of Rouen Cathedral or his late studies of water-lilies are powerful exercizes in pure light and pure color, while Seurat's pictures are composed entirely of tiny dots of color, to be blended in the eye of the beholder.

THE ART OF COLOR

"HARVEST" BY
KAFFE FASSETT
"WATERLEAF" BY
JANICE TCHALENKO

If the colors of nature and light preoccupied the Impressionists, color later began to be used in a very different way by other artists: symbolically as in Gauguin's paintings of the South Seas, or to conjure up a mood, as in the influential work of Whistler. A joy in juxtaposing brilliant expressive colors is evident in the distinctive paintings of Van Gogh. He thought and wrote a great deal about color, believing the artist of the future would be "a colorist such as has never yet been" and characterized his own work as "the search for the high yellow note." Cézanne, rejecting the subjective basis of Impressionism, also used color in an entirely new sense, as a way of expressing what he thought was eternal or essential in the scene before him. The late Impressionists, Bonnard and Vuillard, painted intimate studies of nineteenth-century interiors, steeped in color and dancing with pattern.

By the twentieth century, color was no longer tied to nature, but came from inner feeling, an approach which found its fullest expression with Matisse. His characteristic palette of blue-green, brilliant blue and deep red was the signature of his creative personality. Matisse's paintings rely on color relationships for their structure, and they remain a boundless source of ideas and inspiration for me. Similarly, the often shocking color combinations of the Expressionists such as Kirchner, Nölde, and Munch display profound feeling and intensity.

Delaunay was another artist working in the early twentieth century who gave absolute priority to color. "Color alone is both form and subject," he believed; many of his paintings were essays in color where the subject is almost dissolved. Nature was no longer represented in form or motif, but in pure abstract color relationships. Picasso — perhaps the archetypal twentieth-century artist — progressed from the early Blue and Rose periods characterized by a single defining shade, to the protean color energies of Cubism and beyond.

The Bauhaus, the avant-garde school of modernist art, design, and

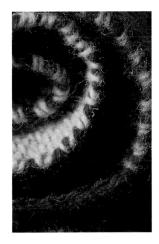

"LARGE FLOWERS" BY
HOWARD HODGKIN.
WOOLLEN THROW BY
RICHARD WOMERSLEY.

architecture which flourished in Germany between the two World Wars, ran courses on color theory taught by Klee and Kandinsky. Their fascinating attempt to come up with a universal visual language related basic forms such as the circle, square, and triangle to primary colors and assigned particular qualities and even sounds to each of the colors in the spectrum.

Past or present, art in all its forms provides new ways of seeing and experiencing color. I have been personally influenced by many painters, from Mark Rothko to David Bomberg. Living artists whose work I find particularly inspiring for their use of color include Frank Auerbach, and Howard Hodgkin. Part of my philosophy at Designers Guild is to work with contemporary artists and I have commissioned both Howard Hodgkin and, more recently, Michael Heindorff, to design textiles for our collections.

Broadening the field from fine art to the decorative arts in general, color is no less a vital element in other areas of creative endeavor, from needlepoint and weaving to ceramics. One of my longest associations with a contemporary craftsman has been with Kaffe Fassett, whose color sense and use of texture in his painterly needlepoints has inspired a whole new generation to experiment with color. The weaver Richard Womersley has also long been associated with Designers Guild. Ceramics are a particular passion, both collecting and working with celebrated ceramicists such as Janice Tchalenko, Carol McNichol and Liz Hodges.

While nature takes us back to basics, art can be a medium for heightening awareness, relating color directly to the expression of feelings and ideas.

THE SCIENCE OF COLOR

Color, in a scientific sense, is how we perceive waves of light. Color is not a quality of an object, it does not reside in anything: in other words, there is no "red" in red shoes. When light strikes an object, the object absorbs all the wavelengths of light except what we see reflected back at us: red shoes, for example, absorb all the wavelengths of light except the red ones, and this is why we see the shoes as red.

Since Newton we have known that white light when broken up by a prism — or waterdrops, as in a rainbow — reveals a continuous spectrum of color, from the longest red wavelengths to the shortest, which are blue. For the sake of convenience, the spectrum is usually represented as six distinct bands of red, orange, yellow, green, blue, and violet. In a color wheel, the ends of the spectrum are brought around to join in a circle.

Although the color wheel is something of an abstract construction, it is useful in helping to understand the effect colors have on each other. Artists such as Van Gogh made deliberate use of the notion of complementary colors in the composition of paintings. (My own response to and use of color is more instinctive, less analytical — and I am a little wary of subjecting what feels essentially personal to scientific analysis!).

At its most simplified, the color wheel consists of the three "primary" colors red, yellow, and blue; the three "secondary" colors orange, green, and violet; and three "tertiary" colors — such as turquoise — which are the colors resulting from equal mixtures of a primary and a secondary. Just as mixing all the colors in the spectrum produces white light, mixing all three primaries would have the same effect.

The color wheel shows very clearly true color relationships. Colors which sit opposite one another are contrasting or "complementary." Complementary pairs — red and green, yellow and violet, orange and blue — mixed together as colored light would give white light. Side by side, they appear to vibrate, a phenomenon which can be put to exciting use in decoration.

MAKING COLOR WORK

Color theory may appear to have little relevance when it comes down to the practical issues of choosing curtain fabric or paint, but a fundamental appreciation of how color works really can help, especially when you are trying to compose a color scheme using more than a couple of colors or variations of one basic shade. Knowing which colors fall into a family that harmonizes naturally, which "vibrate," and why some combinations don't work at all can be of enormous assistance and help to create a vibrant, exciting and original color scheme.

Very fine adjustments can make all the difference. This was underlined for me recently while we were in the process of printing a fabric designed by the artist Michael Heindorff. The print was a complex pattern requiring 21 different screens; as the first sample came off the machines, something looked wrong. The color of the flowers in the original artwork – a particular shade of red – had not been captured, and the image lacked life. With machines running and printers waiting anxiously, I hurriedly scoured a color atlas and eventually found the perfect shade. The change was extraordinary – the balance, light, and quality of the original painting was restored by an infinitesimal alteration in tone.

In a similar way, you can use variables of color tone and saturation to help understand how to put together different combinations. Colors that work in harmony together, such as lighter or darker shades of the same color, are naturally comfortable to the eye, while more exciting and dynamic combinations make use of a pair of complementary but "opposite" colors, such as red and green. By using a fraction of a complementary color as a sharp accent, you can set up more vibrant effects, perhaps offset by an intermediary shade.

Successful color combinations often depend on getting the proportions right. A touch of contrasting color is lively and refreshing; too much can be uncomfortable if blocks of vibrating color are competing for attention.

"STILL LIFE" BY MICHAEL HEINDORFF REPRODUCED AS A FABRIC BY DESIGNERS GUILD.

contemporary convention of decorating bedrooms in light, pastel shades owes something to the elegance of the eighteenth-century French boudoir.

At the end of the eighteenth century, tastes changed and the brilliant colors of European neoclassicism came to the fore. Regency and Empire rooms were often highly colored, and the advances in synthetic pigments at this time meant that bright color was easier to achieve than ever before. The first stable bright yellow came in the 1820s with the development of chrome yellow. Neoclassical schemes, based on archaeological finds at Pompeii and elsewhere, saw rooms decorated in rich reds, yellow, lilac, and a particular shade of green, which, ever since that period, has been associated with the English architect Robert Adam.

Most of us are familiar with the Victorian palette and its rich, somber combinations of magenta, maroon, brown, deep blue, and olive green. A revolution in color occurred in mid-century, when the discovery of synthetic dyes vastly expanded the choice of affordable colors. These new shades were frankly garish compared to the old earth- or vegetable-based colors: new colors included bright pink, mauve, and magenta, named after a Crimean battle. Victorian rooms were multicolored and multipatterned, often quite stifling to modern eyes.

By the late nineteenth century, a reaction to the dull, deep Victorian colors was inevitable. The "greenery-yallery" of the Aesthetics, a color which swept through furnishings and fashion, together with the Arts and Crafts revival of vegetable color, marked a turning point in the use of color in the home.

The twentieth century saw the introduction of the first brilliant white paint when titanium white appeared in the 1920s. After this time, white was suddenly no longer a cheap, utilitarian color, but the height of sophistication in the hands of fashionable society decorators such as Syrie Maugham. Later it became the symbol of architectural purity, and white walls were an essential feature of modernist, minimalist rooms.

COLOR AND CULTURE

VIVID ARCHITECTURAL
DETAIL FROM AROUND
THE WORLD – HAITI,
MOROCCO AND
UZBEKISTAN.

Nowadays, thanks to great strides in the technology of fabric printing and paint manufacture, we take for granted a vast range of colors in decoration – paints that are safe (lead-free), easy to use and widely available – a breadth of choice our ancestors would truly have envied. And today's armchair traveler can not only journey back in time, but also around the world in search of color inspirations. To our Western history of color associations can be added traditions from Mexico, India, Africa and the Far East. The pulsating electric combinations of Central and South America, the wonderful earthy palette of Africa, the subtle neutrals of Japan, the hot swirling pinks and reds of Rajasthan, or the singing ice-cream colors of the Caribbean are becoming as familiar and accessible as Williamsburg blue or Gustavian gray. As the world shrinks, our color horizons broaden.

From these cultural sources, we can really appreciate the excitement of intense color. Unlike the subtle modulations of our traditional decorating palette, these saturated tones are used in sharp contrasts to brighten and enliven houses inside and out. The contrasts may underscore architectural detail, as the deep blues used to pick out frames and borders on Greek-island houses, or simply set up vibrating oppositions. Painted shutters, doors, verandahs, balconies and window frames clash happily with walls in a joyous use of color for its own sake. When resources are limited, luxuries few and far between, the sheer richness of color delights the spirit.

COLOR IN THE INTERIOR

STRONG COLOR GLIMPSED FROM A HALLWAY CREATES A SENSE OF SURPRISE AND INVITATION.

Color is not an abstraction. How we use it in our homes depends on a whole host of factors, including space, proportion, light, and texture.

One persistent decorating convention says that small rooms, particularly small dark rooms, should be decorated in light colors to open them out and make them less confining. This argument is often used to justify decorating halls in neutral shades. I believe, on the contrary, that small rooms can take quite bright colors and that it is far better to accept their limitations and give them a jewel-like brilliance which compensates for the lack of space. In the situation where natural light levels are relatively low, strong color intensifies and becomes richer, which is an added advantage. Warm colors — the reds, yellows, and oranges — are "advancing," and it is this characteristic that makes rooms painted in warm shades seem welcoming and intimate.

Halls, stairs, and connecting areas are places people use frequently, but for limited periods of time, so bright color here can be especially uplifting. The glimpse of a intensely colored hall through an open doorway is inviting; a core of color running from top to bottom draws the whole house together.

The other side of this approach is that in rooms which enjoy a great deal of natural light, light colors emphasize the airy, spacious atmosphere. Pastels or subtly differentiated neutrals can be very reviving in these circumstances.

Another factor to consider when choosing colors is texture. Matt surfaces which absorb light — such as emulsion paint and unglazed cotton — look lighter in color than shiny ones which reflect light — such as polished marble, satin, and glazed chintz.

All color schemes have to start somewhere — a favorite color, or those in a treasured rug, a painting, a piece of pottery; this introduction may have provided some idea of where to look for inspiration. The following chapters focus on individual shades, their associations, folklore, and special qualities; but each color is essentially a starting point for a multiplicity of combinations, which is where the excitement of exploring with color really begins.

WHITE

"AND ALL WOKE EARLIER FOR THE UNACCUSTOMED
BRIGHTNESS OF THE WINTER DAWNING, THE STRANGE
HEAVENLY GLARE: THE EYE MARVELED – MARVELED AT
THE DAZZLING WHITENESS . . .".

LONDON SNOW,
ROBERT BRIDGES

INTRODUCTION

White is a powerful, ancient color. At once ordinary and dynamic, it is the traditional color in the western world for wedding dresses, a symbol of purity and chastity. The color of ghosts and apparitions, white is worn as mourning in Asia; while in Africa, white painted on the outside of dwellings wards off evil.

White interiors are cool and calm. At the same time white rooms are challenging to live in, uncompromising and revealing – an all-white scheme is not the easy option it might at first appear. In such pure surroundings, the emphasis falls on texture; using white can be an exercize in exploring the richness of textural variety. Think of the soft translucence of white marble, the fine nap of freshly washed damask, the delicate filigree of lace, or the crisp taut weave of canvas.

White is naturally a foil for other colors. (In fact, it can be misleading to call white a color at all, since it represents white light, in which all colors are blended.) Used with practically any other shade, white adds a look of freshness. Used with a selection of strong primaries, white can produce a Mondrian-like modernity.

White's classic partner is, of course, its opposite: black. Just as white varies in tone, black can encompass deep midnight blue-black, rusty brown-black, and charcoal — Van Gogh claimed to have identified 27 different shades of black in the paintings of Franz Hals. The monochromatic palette of many of the Dutch masters can be inspirational — lace collars over black velvet, black and white checkered floors. Closer to our time, white and black suggest modernism, the grainy realism of the black and white photograph. Used in small quantities, as a detail, black has the effect of sharpening any color scheme. A basic black and white combination can be very flexible, always offering the potential for dropping in other colors incidentally with the use of flowers or decorative objects, a fluid approach which is well suited to city living. In the same way, using black and white in a kitchen will play on the technology of kitchen equipment and machinery, with the colors of fresh fruit and vegetables providing a contrast.

A HARMONY OF PURE WHITE MAKES A SERENE, CONTEMPLATIVE SPACE IN A HOUSE IN FRANCE.

WHITE LIGHT

WHITE ENLARGES A SPACE AND EMPHASIZES NATURAL LIGHT. IN THIS COOL COUNTRY INTERIOR, THE PLAIN WHITE WALLS, TILED FLOOR, AND DARK WOOD OF THE FURNITURE ARE COMPLEMENTED BY SNOW-WHITE CURTAINS AND THE SIMPLEST TABLECLOTH, ALL EDGED IN A NARROW FRINGED SEERSUCKER BRAID OF DARK BLUE AND WHITE CHECK. THE

SIMPLICITY OF THIS WHITE FURNISHING IS GIVEN LIFT AND SPIRIT BY THE DEFINING LINE OF THE TRIMMING. WHEN COMBINING JUST TWO WHITES – HERE ON WALLS AND IN FABRIC – THEY SHOULD BE BROADLY SIMILAR IN TONE, OTHERWISE THE WARMER VERSION WILL LOOK DISCOLORED BY CONTRAST.

OLD WHITE

SOFT, "DIRTY" WHITES – THE BEAUTIFUL MELLOW WHITES OF DISTEMPER, LIMEWASH, AND WHITEWASH – AGE WELL AND SUIT THE FADED CHARACTER OF WELL-WORN WOOD AND OLD FABRIC. HERE, A LENGTH OF FILMY WHITE COTTON TIED ABOVE THE FRAME MAKES A DELIGHTFUL FLOURISH FOR A WINDOW WHERE SCREENING THE LIGHT IS NOT A PRIORITY (ABOVE LEFT). BY PAINTING THE WOOD PANELING AND BEDHEAD WHITE, A

COOL, DELICATE LOOK WITH WARM, MELLOW UNDERTONES CAN BE ACHIEVED (ABOVE RIGHT). SCANDINAVIA IS THE HOME OF LIGHT, AIRY, PAINTED DECORATION. AND PALE SCRUBBED BOARDS AND DELICATE PAINTED FURNITURE ARE THE ESSENCE OF SCANDINAVIAN COUNTRY STYLE. TO CREATE THIS ATMOSPHERE, USE MATT LATEX TO SIMULATE THE DRY, FLAT PATINA OF OLD PAINTED FINISHES (RIGHT).

CLASSICAL STRIPE

EVEN WITH A MUTED PALETTE OF GRAYS AND WHITES, IT IS STILL POSSIBLE TO ACHIEVE GREAT LIVELINESS AND VARIETY. THE STRENGTH OF THE VARYING GEOMETRIC PRINTS USED ON THE CHAIRS AND STOOLS IS COUNTERBALANCED BY THE CLASSICAL CHARCOAL AND WHITE STRIPED FABRIC WITH BUNCHES OF YELLOW AURICULAS, AND THE IVY PRINT USED TO COVER THE TOP OF A FOOTSTOOL. THERE ARE MANY DIFFERENT SHADES OF WHITE AND ITS NEAR-RELATIVE GRAY: EXPLOIT THESE SUBTLE DIFFERENCES TO CREATE A TIMELESS, CONTEMPLATIVE AND RELAXING MOOD.

BLUE

"BLUE, DARKLY, DEEPLY, BEAUTIFULLY BLUE".

INTRODUCTION

Blue is an ascending color. Like the lift in our spirits when the sky is blue, or the feeling of infinity looking up at the heavens, blue is airy and expansive, generating a supreme sense of well-being. It reminds us of distance, space, sea, and sky.

Perhaps because it is a color which occurs widely in nature, blue is peaceful and refreshing, not tiring or overly exciting. Blue bedrooms are restful, blue bath-rooms suitably watery. Blue was once considered the best color for a kitchen because it was thought to keep flies away, although to our eyes, blue seems at home in the kitchen because of the long decorative tradition of blue and white china and tiles.

Blue is undoubtedly from the "cool" side of the spectrum, but it would be wrong to assume that this means it is invariably cold. The wrong shade of blue in the wrong conditions of light can be uncomfortable, which may well have led to blue's more negative associations with sorrow and gloom. Yet blues vary in-credibly from almost violet to powder blue, from navy to the luminous singing blue of delphiniums.

Natural blue, from the organic vegetable dye indigo was – for many centuries – the only affordable version of the color. The precious mineral lapis lazuli gave an intense blue, but was too expensive for use in the interior: rare and exclusive, it was the special blue of the Madonna's robes in early paintings, signifying her exalted status. Prussian blue, developed in the early eighteenth century, and synthetic blues in the nineteenth, widened, the blue palette.

Blue is valuable in decorating not merely for its fresh, vitalizing qualities, but also because it works so well with many other colors. Blue and white has a tradition of use all its own. Through sheer familiarity it has come to be the most homey of color combinations – the blue and white of countless kitchen plates, mattress ticking, checked gingham. A more electric pairing is the contrast of the opposites blue and yellow. Whether the combination is grand dark blue patterned with gold stars or sky blue accented with lemon yellow, the effect is invigorating. And blues acquire depth in combination with greens and reds.

INTEGRAL SHELVES AND KITCHEN DRESSER IN A PRUSSIAN BLUE – A SURPRISING CHOICE FOR THIS BRETON HOUSE.

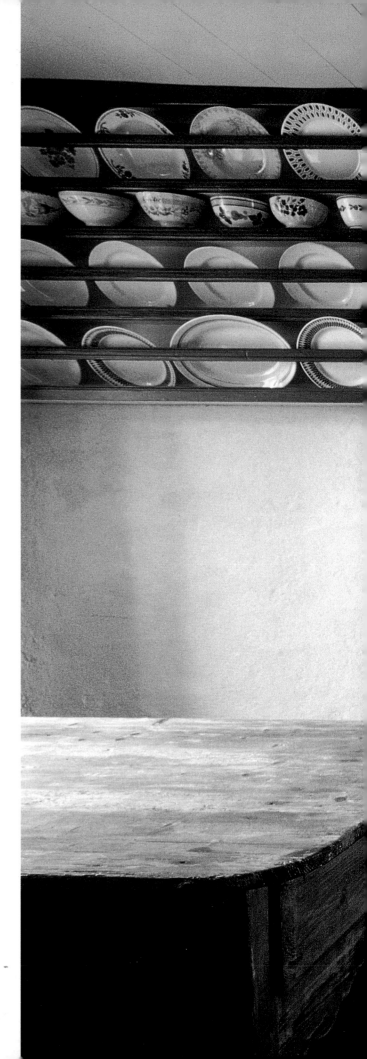

FRENCH BLUE

THE ELEGANCE OF NATURAL BLUE, LIKE INDIGO WHICH FADES TO A SOFT WARM COLOR, IS DISPLAYED IN THIS FRENCH BEDROOM WITH ITS TIME-WORN BLUE-GRAY PANELING. THE CAST-IRON BED HAS A COVERLET IN A BOLD, TEXTURED STRIPE, WHICH COMBINES EFFORTLESSLY WITH THE PAINTERLY CHECK FABRIC USED FOR PILLOWCASES AND CHAIR COVERING. AT THE TALL WINDOW, A DROP OF FABRIC VERTICALLY BANDED WITH A CLASSICALLY STYLIZED DESIGN ADDS SOPHISTICATION TO THE COMPOSITION. THE THREE FABRICS WORK WELL BECAUSE, ASIDE FROM THEIR COMMON COLORS, EACH HAS AN INHERENTLY GEOMETRIC STRUCTURE. WHEN PLACING DIFFERENT PATTERNS TOGETHER, THERE SHOULD ALWAYS BE SOME BASIC AFFINITY BETWEEN THE DESIGNS.

GUSTAVIAN GRAY

THE FAMILY OF GRAY-BLUES AND BLUE-GRAYS IS STRONGLY ASSOCIATED WITH THE GUSTAVIAN PERIOD OF EIGHTEENTH-CENTURY SWEDEN. SCANDINAVIAN DECORATION OF ALL ERAS DEMONSTRATES A LOVE OF LIGHT, AND THE PARTICULAR ATTRACTION OF THESE COOL SHADES IS THAT THEY ENHANCE NATURAL LIGHT AND BRIGHTEN ROOMS.

A PAINTED BLUE CHAIR, BLUE CLOSET DOORS, AND STRIPED BEDHANGINGS MAKE SIMPLE AND FRESH BEDROOM DECORATION (ABOVE). THE IDIOSYNCRATIC WALLPAINTING IN AN EIGHTEENTH-CENTURY SWEDISH INTERIOR IS SET OFF BY RICH BLUE-GRAY DADOS AND DOORWAYS, EFFECTIVE BECAUSE OF THE SHEER REPETITION OF COLOR (RIGHT).

CHECKS AND SPOTS

BLUE AND WHITE LOOK BEST WHEN USED IN THE FORM OF COOL GEOMETRIC DESIGNS IN SPOTS, STRIPES AND CHECKS, LIVELY PATTERNS WHICH CAN BE LAYERED IN HUNDREDS OF DIFFERENT COMBINATIONS – THE SIMPLEST AND MOST FOOLPROOF FORM OF PATTERN MIXING. THE VARIETY OF MOODS AND EFFECTS THAT CAN BE ACHIEVED BY COMBINING THESE TWO COLOURS IS SEEMINGLY ENDLESS, FROM PRETTY DELICATE SPOTTED DESIGNS TO FORTHRIGHT CHECKS, FRESH AND UPLIFTING.

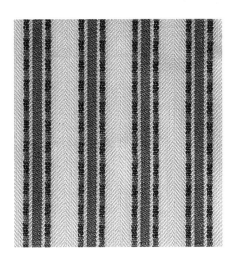

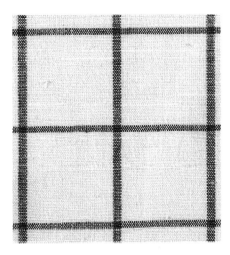

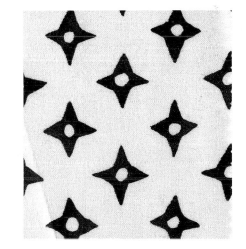

BLUE AND WHITE

A CLASSIC COMBINATION, BLUE AND WHITE IS REFRESHING, CHARMING, AND UTTERLY HARMONIOUS. THE FASHION FOR BLUE AND WHITE DECORATION PROBABLY DATES FROM THE SEVENTEENTH CENTURY WHEN CHINESE PORCELAIN BEGAN ARRIVING IN QUANTITIES IN THE WESTERN WORLD. TODAY THIS PARTNERSHIP SUGGESTS EVERYDAY USE MORE THAN EXOTIC DECORATION – TILES, DISHES, AND TICKING – BUT IS NO LESS POWERFUL OR APPEALING. DELFT TILES AND PORTUGUESE *AZULEJOS* ARE TWO EXAMPLES OF BLUE AND WHITE TILE TRADITIONS, WHILE PERHAPS THE FINEST OF ALL CERAMIC ART DATES FROM SIXTEENTH-CENTURY ISTANBUL WHERE BLUE AND WHITE, AND TURQUOISE TILES EMBELLISHED EVERY SURFACE OF MOSQUES AND PALACES. IN FABRIC, THE BLUE AND WHITE COMBINATION LENDS ITSELF TO GEOMETRIC DESIGNS OF CHECKS.

LAVENDER BLUE

MAUVE, LAVENDER AND ICE BLUE ARE COOL, REFRESHING COLORS, MUCH ENHANCED BY WHITE. AND IT IS IN THIS COMBINATION THAT THESE PARTICULAR SHADES OF BLUE ARE MOST OFTEN SEEN, DECORATING THE OUTSIDES OF HOUSES FROM NORTH AFRICA TO GREECE, REFLECTING LIGHT WITH A DAZZLING INTENSITY. LAVENDER, WITH ITS WARM UNDERTONES OF RED, IS THE LIGHTEST AND EASIEST OF THE COLOR FAMILY BASED ON MIXTURES OF BLUE AND RED. PURPLE

CAN BE NOTORIOUSLY DIFFICULT TO HANDLE THOUGH. ONCE SO RARE AND PRECIOUS, ITS USE WAS EXCLUSIVELY RESERVED FOR IMPERIAL ROBES. EVEN TODAY THE COLOR HAS NOT QUITE LOST THESE ELEVATED ASSOCIATIONS. LAVENDER, ON THE OTHER HAND, IS AS FRESH AND COUNTRIFIED AS ITS NAME. SOOTHING, SHARP AND VITALIZING, IT LOOKS GOOD PLACED AGAINST ITS NATURAL PARTNER WHITE, OR USED WITH ACCENTS OF YELLOW AND GREEN.

ITALIAN CHECK

FURNISHING FABRICS IN THE FORM OF FITTED COVERS OR UPHOLSTERY CAN BE AN IMPORTANT MEANS OF INJECTING COLOR IN TO AN ESSENTIALLY NEUTRAL ROOM, WHERE WALLS ARE WHITE AND FLOORS ARE NATURAL WOOD OR TILE. THE SINGING CONTRAST OF CLEAR YELLOW AND COBALT BLUE UNITES A GROUP OF CHECKED AND STRIPED FABRICS. THE VIBRANT COMBINATION OF BLUE AND YELLOW IS PARTICULARLY INVIGORATING IN STRONG LIGHT AND OFFERS A GREAT DEAL OF DECORATIVE POTENTIAL. THE COLORS CAN BE SET OFF AGAINST EACH OTHER WHILE BALANCED WITHIN THE SAME GEOMETRIC PRINT, OR USED AS BLOCKS OF SOLID COLOR, OR SEEN IN UNEQUAL PROPORTIONS WITH ONE COLOR AS SHARP ACCENT TRIMMING FOR A MAIN FABRIC.

BLUE AND YELLOW

THIS IS AN ELECTRIC, NATURAL PARTNERSHIP: THE SUN
IN A SUMMER SKY, THE YELLOW CENTER OF A BLUE
FLOWER, BRIGHT SUNLIGHT DAPPLED ON WATER.
PERSIAN MINIATURES EMBELLISHED WITH GOLD AND
LAPIS LAZULI, AND MEDIEVAL BOOKS OF HOURS WITH
GILDED LETTERING AND RICH, GLOWING BLUE
BACKGROUNDS, SHOW THE DAZZLING RICHNESS OF
THE COMBINATION. AT THE SAME TIME, WHEN BLUE
AND YELLOW ARE MIXED TOGETHER, THEY PRODUCE
GREEN AND THE CENTRAL HARMONY AND BALANCE OF
THIS COLOR IS IMPLICIT IN BLUE AND YELLOW SCHEMES.
ULTRAMARINE AND GOLD, SKY BLUE AND SUNSHINE
YELLOW, LIGHT BLUE AND PRIMROSE, WHEAT GOLD
AND DUCK-EGG, THE MOST SUCCESSFUL PAIRINGS OF
THE TWO COLORS ARE THOSE WHICH MATCH TONALLY.

AQUAMARINE

THE INTRIGUING SHADE OF AQUAMARINE, THE COLOR
OF THE WATER OVER THE SHELVING SEA FLOOR, IS
WHERE BLUE MEETS GREEN. BOLD AND COMPELLING,
YET RESTFUL AT THE SAME TIME, IT IS A SHADE OFTEN
FOUND IN COUNTRIES WHERE THE LIGHT IS BRIGHT AND
STRONG, SOMETIMES PAINTED ON THE LOWER HALF OF
THE WALL AS A DADO WITH WHITEWASH APPLIED OVER
THE UPPER PORTION OF THE WALL. NEITHER COOL NOR
NEUTRAL, THIS BLUE IS A CHALLENGING COLOR FOR A
LIVING ROOM OR BEDROOM, STIMULATING BUT NOT
TIRING ON THE EYE. A BOLD VERSION OF THE COLOR IS
TYPICAL OF TUNISIAN DECORATION; THE JOLTING
COLOR CONTRASTS OF NORTH AFRICA HAVE PROVIDED
INSPIRATION FOR MANY TWENTIETH-CENTURY ARTISTS,
NOTABLY PAUL KLEE AND MATISSE.

BLUE AND GREEN

"BLUE AND GREEN SHOULD NEVER BE SEEN..." IS ONE FOLK SAYING THAT MAKES VERY LITTLE SENSE. BLUE AND GREEN ARE SEEN EVERYWHERE TOGETHER. WHERE SKY MEETS GREEN HILLS OR SEASCAPE, THE SPECTRUM FROM VIOLET TO BLUE TO AQUAMARINE TO GREEN BLENDS EFFORTLESSLY. THE EDGINESS OF THE TWO COLORS HAS LONG BEEN A SOURCE OF FASCINATION, ESPECIALLY THE VARIETY OF BLUE-GREENS, FROM JADE TO TURQUOISE AND SEAGREEN. TURQUOISE, A POWERFUL ANCIENT COLOR MUCH PRIZED IN TIBET, ALSO INTRIGUED THE EGYPTIANS, INCAS, AND PERSIANS. APOTHECARY BLUE, A PALE BLUE-GREEN, WAS A FAVORITE COLOR OF FEDERAL AMERICA; A MUCH BRIGHTER VERSION OF THE COLOR IS SHOWN IN THE INTERIOR OF MOUNT VERNON, GEORGE WASHINGTON'S HOME (CENTER TOP).

GREEN

"IN MUSIC, ABSOLUTE GREEN IS REPRESENTED BY THE PLACID, MIDDLE NOTES OF A VIOLIN".

ANALOGIES OF COLORS AND MUSIC,

WASSILY KANDINSKY

INTRODUCTION

Green represents balance and harmony. The product of total opposites blue and yellow, green is the color of the landscape, the national color of Ireland, and the holy color of Islam. In many cultures, green is symbolic of the natural cycle of life and death – the Folkloric English "Green Man" and the Egyptian god of death, green-faced Osiris, both refer to this powerful connection. We mark the association more prosaically in the names we give different shades of green – leaf, olive, mint, grass, apple, lime. In counterpart to these associations are the negative connotations – green as the color of envy and jealousy, or even betrayal, and the green of the serpent.

Green can also be elegant and sophisticated. The jade greens and celadons of the East, as well as neo-classical Adam greens, are extremely subtle colors, more suggestive of culture and refinement than of the glories of nature. The Aesthete movement at the end of the nineteenth century adopted a particular shade of yellow-green, promptly satirized by Gilbert and Sullivan as "greenery-yallery," as a symbol of their precious artistic sensitivities.

Green is easy on the eye. At one time green was thought to be beneficial for the eyesight, and sunblinds made of green fabric were a common way of filtering strong light. Similarly, green was used as a traditionally contemplative background for a library or study. Aside from these specific applications, green has a long history of use in the interior, on paneling and woodwork, as well as fabric and furnishings. While green is most peaceful and perhaps most versatile in soft, muted shades, bright vibrant greens were an outstanding feature of Empire rooms, a fashion fostered by Napoleon.

Just as many greens are found together in nature, most shades of green harmonize effortlessly, from fir green to sea green, gray-green to emerald. Green and white are another natural pair, delicate and countrified. Green and red are complementaries which work together in many interesting ways. Forest green and tomato red possess a cheerful folk-art quality; lighter greens and light reds or rose are also highly compatible.

TIMEWORN GREEN PANELING MAKES A MELLOW BACKGROUND FOR THIS SCANDINAVIAN FARMHOUSE.

PISTACHIO

A LIGHT, COOL, RESTFUL GREEN IS A GOOD CHOICE FOR A BACKGROUND IN A BEDROOM THAT RECEIVES MORNING SUN. REFRESHING AND VITAL, THIS PARTICULAR SHADE OF GREEN IS RATHER SHARPER THAN THE FAMOUS CELADON ASSOCIATED WITH THE PORCELAIN OF THE SUNG DYNASTY OF CHINA, BUT IS EQUALLY VERSATILE. THE CEILING AND FLOOR ARE LIGHT TO MAINTAIN THE AIRY QUALITY OF THE ROOM. BLACK-AND-WHITE CHECKED UPHOLSTERY ON THE BED AND STOOL GIVES A GRAPHIC BASE TO THE LIME, SAFFRON, AND PURPLE CONTRASTS OF THE FABRIC USED TO COVER THE BED.

FOREST GREEN

A ROOM DECORATED ALL IN SHADES OF GREEN COULD NEVER BE DULL OR DISCORDANT – THE GREENS OF NATURE VARY FROM THE DEEP FIR GREEN OF SPRUCE TREES TO THE BRIGHT YELLOW-GREEN OF NEW SPRING GROWTH, FROM SILVERY GRAY ROSEMARY TO EMERALD TURF. CITRUS YELLOW AND FIR GREEN ARE A TRADITIONAL INTERIOR COMBINATION THAT BOASTS RATHER NORDIC ASSOCIATIONS, ESPECIALLY WHEN DISPLAYED IN THE FORM OF A BOLD CHECKED PRINT (LEFT).

GARDEN

IN THE GARDEN, GREEN IS THE ANCHORING COLOR, THE FOIL FOR EYE-CATCHING SHADES OF FLOWERS AND FRUIT. IN THIS FARMHOUSE BEDROOM WITH ITS RAFTERED CEILING, ALL THE SOFT TONALITIES OF THE FLOWER GARDEN ARE DISPLAYED IN THE COMBINATION OF WILLOW, FIR, AND LIME GREENS, SET AGAINST WARMER ROSE AND GOLDEN YELLOWS. THE BIG-SCALE FRUIT PATTERN ON THE FACING CURTAINS HAS A WATERCOLOR TRANSPARENCY WHICH SOFTENS THE BOLDNESS OF THE DESIGN. BLUE-AND-WHITE UNDERCURTAINS ECHO THE GEOMETRIC UPHOLSTERY OF THE CHAIR. HAVING TWO PAIRS OF CURTAINS AT THE WINDOW MEANS ONE LIGHT-FILTERING SET CAN BE DRAWN WHEN THE SUN IS STRONG, WITH A FACING OUTER CURTAIN RESERVED FOR SHEER DECORATIVE INTEREST.

84 GREEN

SEASHORE

VIBRATING SHADES OF SEA GREEN AND LUMINOUS BLUE ARE FOUND ON THE SEASHORES OF THE MEDITERRANEAN AND CARIBBEAN, THE CHEERFUL OPPOSITION OF COLOR PARTICULARLY BRILLIANT IN THE CLARITY OF THE LIGHT. GREEK ISLAND HOUSES ARE OFTEN WHITEWASHED, OR COLORWASHED IN FADED OCHERS, WITH DETAIL – DOORS, WINDOW FRAMES, AND SHUTTERS – PAINTED IN SOFT, BRIGHT GREENS, BLUES, AND GRAYS. WATER-BASED VERSIONS OF THIS MEDITERRANEAN PALETTE ARE AVAILABLE AND EASY TO USE; COLORS CAN BE READILY THINNED TO THE REQUIRED DEGREE OF INTENSITY (LEFT). CARIBBEAN COLOR SENSE, DISPLAYED IN THE PAINTING OF THIS HAITIAN BEACHHOUSE, IS EXUBERANT AND FULL OF GAIETY, ITS BRIGHT CHALKY COLORS SHOW UP IN THE SUNSHINE (RIGHT).

86 GREEN

APPLE GREEN

A RUSTIC LOOK FOR A
DINING ROOM TEAMS A
WALLPAPER AND BORDER AT
DADO LEVEL WITH
CURTAINS IN A LARGE-
SCALE GARLAND PRINT. THE
SATURATED COLORS OF
SHARP GREEN AND
GOLDEN YELLOW
MEDIATED BY RUSSET MAKE
A MELLOW BACKGROUND
FOR AN EATING ROOM,
WHERE THE ATMOSPHERE
CAN BE SOMEWHAT
THEATRICAL AND THE
QUALITY OF LIGHT ADDS TO
THE ENJOYMENT OF FOOD
AND CONVERSATION. A
STRICT COORDINATION OF
PAPER AND FABRIC CAN BE
DEADENING, WHEREAS THE
SUBTLE VARIATIONS IN
THESE DESIGNS,
REFLECTING THEIR
DIFFERENT APPLICATIONS,
IS MORE INTERESTING.

CHUTNEY

THE SPICY COMBINATION OF LIME AND MANGO
INSPIRES A LIVELY MIXTURE OF PATTERN IN A BEDROOM.
BEDS OFFER GREAT POTENTIAL FOR CONTRIBUTING
COLOR AND PATTERN INTEREST: BED COVERS, THROWS,
QUILTS, AND BLANKETS CAN DISPLAY A SYMPHONY OF
HARMONIZING AND CONTRASTING SHADES FAR FROM
THE BLAND AND NEUTRAL APPEARANCE OF PLAIN
BEDSPREADS OR QUILT COVERS. FURTHER DRESSING IN
THE FORM OF BOLSTER COVERS, PILLOWCASES, AND
THROW-PILLOW COVERS REINFORCES THE FURNISHED
LOOK, MAKING THE BEDROOM A PLACE TO RELAX IN AT
ALL TIMES OF THE DAY.

GREEN 91

AUTHENTIC GREEN

GREEN IN ALL OF ITS VARIATIONS HAS BEEN ONE OF THE MOST PREVALENT COLORS IN THE HISTORY OF DECORATION, EACH SHADE ASSOCIATED WITH A CHARACTERISTIC PERIOD OR STYLE. DEEP FIR GREEN WAS A COMMON COLOR FOR GEORGIAN PANELING; BRIGHTER PEA GREEN DATES FROM LATER IN THE EIGHTEENTH CENTURY. ROBERT ADAM MADE USE OF A VARIETY OF LIGHT GREENS AND BLUE-GREENS, WITH DIFFERENT SHADES DEFINING CHANGES IN MODELING AND MOLDING. YELLOW-GREEN WAS AN IMPORTANT FEDERAL COLOR, WHILE BRILLIANT GREEN WAS FAVORED BY NAPOLEON AND WIDELY SEEN IN EMPIRE ROOMS. THE VICTORIANS ENJOYED MORE SOMBER GREENS AND OLIVE SHADES, WITH A DULL VEGETABLE GREEN BEING PARTICULARLY ASSOCIATED WITH THE LATE NINETEENTH-CENTURY ARTS AND CRAFTS MOVEMENT. ALL SHADES OF TRADITIONAL GREEN LEND AN AIR OF REST AND RELAXATION TO BOTH LIVING ROOMS AND BEDROOMS.

YELLOW

"THE MAGIC OF THE SUN TRANSMUTES THE PALM TREES INTO GOLD, THE WATER SEEMS FULL OF DIAMONDS AND MEN BECOME KINGS FROM THE EAST".

PIERRE AUGUSTE RENOIR,

WRITING OF ALGERIA

INTRODUCTION

Yellow is warm and enriching. The color of sunlight, buttercups, lemons, and gold, it draws the eye. It is inescapably cheerful, a bright uplifting color that always strikes a positive note without becoming too insistent.

Like other colors, it has its special meanings. The saffron of monks' robes is a holy color in Buddhism; while yellow's natural associations with the power of the sun and ripening grain make it a necessary part of harvest celebrations. Yellow (and its near-relative orange) are most notable for being particularly eye-catching, which goes some way to explaining their widespread use in packaging, graphics, and signs — any application where being noticed quickly is of the utmost importance.

In decoration, yellow — in its pure, clear form — was unknown before the manufacture of chrome yellow at the beginning of the nineteenth century, although quite surprisingly bright yellows using the earth pigment ocher were achieved before this time. The arrival of chrome yellow coincided with the neoclassical taste for brilliant color; bright yellow was also a signature Empire color.

One of the best known of all yellow rooms is Monet's dining room at his home in Giverny, France. The singing yellow walls give the effect of drenching the room with sunlight and make a vivid background for Monet's collection of Japanese prints. The clever combination of subtle and strong yellow tones at Giverny has provided inspiration for countless decorators. Equally influential in its dramatic use of yellow was the London drawing room of Nancy Lancaster, decorated in the 1950s in a warm rich shade of yellow which the American decorator nicknamed "buttah yellah." The strength and appeal of this color scheme set a whole new fashion in English country-house style.

Yellow lightens and brightens any room. Traditionally a kitchen color, where its natural vivacity promotes a cozy feeling of hospitality, it can also be a good choice for a bedroom, particularly one that gets the early morning sun. On the other hand, a room that looks out on a dull, gray city street might benefit enormously from a yellow-based scheme to counteract the lack of light. Light primrose yellows work well with grays and whites. The deeper versions of the color stand up better in stronger combinations. Pure lemon yellow is a natural accompaniment to blues; the warmer mellow yellows can be beautifully complemented with crimsons and roses.

MONET'S FAMOUS DINING ROOM AT GIVERNY COMBINES PURE SUNSHINE
YELLOW WITH FORGET-ME-KNOT BLUE TO OUTSTANDING EFFECT.

CHROME YELLOW

REALLY BRIGHT YELLOW WAS FIRST MANUFACTURED IN THE EARLY DECADES OF THE NINETEENTH CENTURY AND RAPIDLY GAINED FAVOR. IN THE INTERIORS OF NEOCLASSICAL BRITISH ARCHITECTS SUCH AS SIR JOHN SOANE, IT WAS COMBINED WITH BLACK AND WARM RED, AND THIS CONTEMPORARY SCHEME MAKES USE OF THE SAME DYNAMIC COMBINATION TO GREAT EFFECT. THE SELF-STRIPE OF THE FABRIC ON SOFA AND SCREEN HAS A GENTLY MODULATING EFFECT ON THE BLOCKS OF SOLID COLOR, WITH THE SMALL TERRACOTTA FRINGE ADDING A SUITABLY COMPLEMENTARY TOUCH. THE PAIRING OF YELLOW AND BLACK HAS AN ESPECIALLY MODERN GRAPHIC QUALITY. BRIGHT COLOR CAN BE A GOOD CHOICE FOR A HALLWAY, ENLIVENING AN OTHER-WISE "LOST" AND CHARACTERLESS SPACE AND RUNNING LIKE A VIVID THREAD FROM LEVEL TO LEVEL, CONNECTING ROOMS AND VIEWS.

OCHER

EARTH YELLOWS, DERIVED FROM OCHER AND RAW SIENNA, HAVE A LONG HISTORY OF USE AROUND THE WORLD. ALTHOUGH THEY CAN BE SURPRISINGLY BRIGHT, LIKE OTHER EARTH COLORS THEY NEVER ACHIEVE THE LUMINOSITY OF A TRUE PRIMARY. LIVELY AND WARM, EARTH YELLOWS MAKE EXCELLENT WALL COLORS, SOFTENING THE LIGHT AND PROVIDING A GLOWING BACKGROUND FOR OTHER FURNISHING COLORS. DERIVED LITERALLY FROM EARTH – FROM CLAY AND SAND – THESE PIGMENTS HAVE ALWAYS BEEN EASY TO FIND, HENCE THEIR WIDESPREAD USE, FROM AFRICA TO NORTHERN EUROPE. IN THIS GUJARAT MUD HUT ARE DELIGHTFUL SAFFRON-COVERED BEDS (ABOVE) AND NATURALLY WORN OCHER-WASHED WALLS (RIGHT).

GOLD

THE QUALITY OF LIGHT CAN MAKE AN IMPORTANT DIFFERENCE TO THE WAY IN WHICH YELLOW IS PERCEIVED. LATE AFTERNOON LIGHT WITH ITS WARM GOLD TONES LENDS A SPECIAL RICHNESS TO THE MIXTURE OF BRIGHT YELLOW, GREEN AND TOUCHES OF RED AND BLUE. SOPHISTICATED AND LIGHT-ENHANCING, YELLOW IS OFTEN BEST DISPLAYED IN LARGER ROOMS, SUCH AS THIS DRAWING ROOM WITH ITS MELLOW PANELING AND TALL WINDOW. THE SWATHE OF FABRIC PATTERNED WITH GARLANDS OF FRUIT BLENDS COMFORTABLY WITH THE SELF-STRIPED YELLOW OF THE LOOSE COVERING ON THE CHAIR. THE MEREST HINT OF RED AND BLUE ALONGSIDE YELLOW IN THE OTHER STRIPED FABRIC ON THE SOFA GIVES DEPTH AND BALANCE TO THE PRINT.

FEDERAL YELLOW

LIGHT PRIMROSE YELLOW, AS WELL AS A STRONGER YELLOW-GREEN, WERE MUCH USED IN THE INTERIORS OF COLONIAL AND FEDERAL AMERICA. COLOR IS AN IMPORTANT MEANS OF EXPRESSING AND ENHANCING RICH ARCHITECTURAL DETAIL, AS THE VIEW OF A SPLENDID EIGHTEENTH-CENTURY HALL IN HOMEWOOD HOUSE, BALTIMORE, DISPLAYS. THE WHITE COVED CEILING AND CRISP MOLDINGS ARE THROWN INTO RELIEF BY THE FRESH YELLOW WALLS AND PALE DUCK-EGG BLUE DETAIL (RIGHT). PRIMROSE AND MINT- STRIPED CURTAINS UNDER A FACING CURTAIN IN A FLOWERED STRIPE ADD FLAIR TO A SEATING AREA (LEFT).

YELLOW AND BLUE

YELLOW AND BLUE IS AN UPLIFTING COMBINATION, THE COLORS OF SUNNY SUMMER DAYS. YELLOW WARMS AND BRIGHTENS, WHILE BLUE IS EXPANSIVE AND AIRY, MAKING A VERSATILE, STABLE PARTNERSHIP FOR ANY INTERIOR. THIS COLOR COMBINATION CAN ALSO BE SUCCESSFUL OUTDOORS. A CANE-SEATED CHAIR PAINTED BLUE SINGS OUT AGAINST WALLPAPER PATTERNED WITH MELLOW FRUIT FULL OF SUN, A WARM COMBINATION OF COLORS TYPICAL OF PROVENCE (RIGHT). SIMPLER, BUT NO LESS EFFECTIVE, IS THE ELECTRIC OPPOSITION OF THE TWO COLORS IN THE PAINTED WALL AND BALCONY (ABOVE).

CITRUS

SHARP YELLOWS AND GREENS – THE CITRUS COLORS
OF LEMON AND LIME – HAVE ALL THE FRESHNESS OF
EARLY SUMMER. MEDIATED BY WHITE, THEY FORM A
VERSATILE COMBINATION, IDEAL FOR BRIGHT ROOMS
WHICH RECEIVE A GOOD DEAL OF NATURAL LIGHT.
CRISP AND TAILORED IN STRIPES, LEMON, LIME AND
WHITE HAVE A MORE TRADITIONAL ASSOCIATION IN
RAVISHING CHINTZES. MAINTAIN THE HARMONY BY
COMBINING SHADES WHICH ARE EQUAL IN TONAL
STRENGTH: MIX BRIGHT WITH BRIGHT AND
JUXTAPOSE PALE WITH PALE FOR A GOOD EFFECT.

TUSCAN GLOW

THE SATURATED TONES OF ITALIAN LIGHT, FAMOUSLY WARM AND GOLDEN, ARE ECHOED IN THE CHOICE OF COLORS IN THIS *AL FRESCO* SEATING AREA. THE BLEND OF YELLOW AND PINK ON THE DAY BED RELATE TO THE WARM PLASTER PINK OF THE WALL, WHILE A LIGHT GREEN SERVES AS THE ACCENT, A FESTIVE MIXTURE OF SUMMER COLORS. FOR THE ECONOMICALLY MINDED, THROW PILLOWS ARE A GOOD WAY OF INTRODUCING A VARIETY OF PATTERNS AND COLORS THAT ARE SUITABLE FOR EACH SEASON OF THE YEAR.

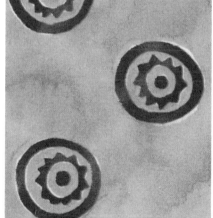

YELLOW 115

YELLOW AND PINK

YOU MAY BE FORGIVEN FOR THINKING THAT SUCH STARTLING COMBINATIONS AS BRILLIANT-YELLOW AND MAGENTA COULD ONLY BE A PRODUCT OF THE MODERN SYNTHETIC WORLD. IT MAY BE SURPRISING, THEN, TO FIND THAT NATURE PROVIDES COLOR SHOCKS THAT ARE EVERY BIT AS THRILLING AND SPECTACULAR AS THOSE CONCOCTED BY A

COMMERCIAL PAINT MANUFACTURER. YELLOW AND PINK, AS SEEN IN THE BALINESE DISPLAY OF BOTTLES (LEFT), OR THE CLOSE-UP OF A GERBERA'S CENTER (RIGHT), HAVE AMAZING VITALITY TOGETHER. TO MAKE THIS COLOR COMBINATION WORK IN THE INTERIOR, MEDIATE THE SCHEME WITH A SHARP LIGHT GREEN.

NATURAL

"THE COLORIST IS HE WHO SEEING A COLOR IN NATURE
KNOWS AT ONCE HOW TO ANALYZE IT, AND CAN SAY
FOR INSTANCE: THAT GREEN-GRAY IS YELLOW WITH

INTRODUCTION

Nature abounds with color, but the true natural palette encompasses a wonderfully subtle variety of creams, gray-browns, and biscuit shades, the colors of wood, stone, and earth. Our enthusiasm for these warm neutrals has much to do with today's increasing appreciation of natural materials and ethnic craftwork. The traditional Japanese house, with its golden tatami mats and ricepaper screens, has been an important influence in this quest for natural simplicity.

Natural colors have long been the mainstay of home decoration. Buffs and browns are among the most widely used and accessible of all colors, readily available from earth pigments such as ochers and umbers. The appropriately termed "drab" was a standard interior color of the eighteenth and nineteenth century. Grays and creams reminiscent of weathered stone were also popular in English Georgian houses. Brown was the color for woodwork — doors, dados, and paneling were painted naturalistically in "wood" colors, an odd notion today when "wood" colors are more likely to come from the natural material.

Natural color schemes have an inherent simplicity. Rush mats or coir on the floor, earthenware pots, unbleached calico and muslin, nubbly raw linens and silks, wickerwork, and waxed wood have a pleasing textural variety that adds interest to the muted color range. Yet natural colors can also be highly sophisticated. Using a range of narrowly differentiated shades to pick out architectural detailing – ceiling molding or plasterwork modeling, for example – was an approach much favored by John Fowler in his color schemes for grand English houses.

Natural colors often work best on their own without the introduction of brighter, more saturated shades. But there is enough choice and depth within the family of neutrals for this hardly to be a restriction; texture extends the scope still further. Walls painted in warm natural or muddied colors can be set off crisply by pure white ceilings and woodwork; black detailing can also give a sharp graphic edge. The best strong colors to accompany a natural scheme have some earthy quality to them as well – brick or Indian reds and warm indigo blues will not overwhelm the essential softness.

There are few rooms which will not suit this type of color scheme. Natural rooms are restful, if rather retiring; there is an added freshness and simplicity which can be very appealing in bedrooms, living rooms, and kitchens alike. A positive advantage is the opportunity to explore different materials, from quarry tiles and limed oak, to sisal and slate, and to enjoy the intrinsic beauty of the naturally occurring materials.

THE SOFT NATURAL TONES FROM CREAM TO BUFF, SUBTLE AND COMFORTABLE, HAVE BEEN USED IN DECORATION FOR CENTURIES.

DRIFTWOOD

THE SANDY COLORS OF
NORTHERN SHORES,
BLEACHED BY SUN AND SEA,
MAKE UP A NATURALLY
HARMONIOUS FAMILY. THE
COUNTRIFIED SIMPLICITY
OF WHITE WALLS AND TILED
FLOOR HAS BEEN CARRIED
OVER INTO THE STYLE OF
FURNISHING, WITH A
SAND-AND-BLACK
CHECKED PATTERN USED TO
COVER A CHAIR AND A
SIMILAR RUST-AND-BISCUIT
CHECKED FABRIC
CURTAINING A DOORWAY
BENEATH A FACING
DRAPERY OF MUTED STONE
COLORS. IMPORTANT
ELEMENTS ARE THE BLACK
DETAILS IN THE CHAIR
UPHOLSTERY AND CURTAIN
FRINGING, WHICH ADD
STRENGTH TO THE SOFT
TONAL RANGE. CURTAINS
FOR DOORWAYS – ONCE
CALLED *PORTIÈRES* – MAKE
SENSE IN WARM AND COOL
CLIMATES ALIKE. IN
NORTHERN COUNTRIES,
THEY PROVIDE EXCELLENT
INSULATION AGAINST
DRAFTS, IN WARM AREAS OF
THE WORLD, THEY SCREEN
STRONG LIGHT AND HELP
KEEP INTERIORS COOL.

NATURE STUDY

BROWN IS TOO PLAIN A TERM FOR THE RICH TONES OF
WOOD, STONE, AND EARTH WHICH MAKE UP THE
NATURAL PALETTE. A STRIP OF BARK, A PIECE OF
DRIFTWOOD, CORN COBS, WEATHERED CARVING, OLD
STONE WALLS – YOU CAN LOOK AT ANY ONE OF A
NUMBER OF NATURAL MATERIALS AND SEE A WEALTH OF
DISTINCT SHADES AND NUANCES OF TONE FROM
CHARCOAL TO BUFF, TOBACCO BROWN TO BISCUIT.
ALL OF THESE SHADES HAVE A LONG HISTORY OF USE IN
THE INTERIOR. BROWNS OF VARIOUS HUES WERE THE
TRADITIONAL COLORS FOR DOORS AND WOODWORK;
LIGHTER BUFFS AND "DRAB" NATURAL SHADES WERE
COMMON WALL COLORS FOR SEVERAL CENTURIES. SET
AGAINST SPARKLING WHITE DETAIL AND A HINT OF
BLACK FOR DEPTH, THEY HAVE THE POWER TO CREATE
ROOMS OF EXCEPTIONAL REFINEMENT AND
UTMOST RESTFULNESS.

FRESCO

THE WARM BUFF COLOR OF NATURAL PLASTER IS THE IDEAL BACKGROUND FOR A
DINING ROOM. THE COLOR LOOKS SOFT AND TRANQUIL WITH DAYLIGHT
STREAMING THRU FRENCH WINDOWS; AT NIGHT, UNDER CANDLELIGHT, IT
COMES ALIVE, WITH THE GLOWING COLORS OF FOOD SINGING OUT IN
CONTRAST. SUCH NEUTRAL TONES, NEITHER ENCLOSING NOR RETREATING,
CREATE AN ATMOSPHERE OF SPACE AND LIGHT IDEAL FOR AN EATING ROOM.
PLAIN PLASTER CAN BE TOO PINK IN ITS UNTREATED STATE, AND MUST BE SEALED
IN ANY CASE BECAUSE DUST FORMS ON ITS SURFACE. A TONING WASH OR
GLAZE GIVES DEPTH WITHOUT LOSING THE NATURAL COLOR.

TERRACOTTA

"GIVE ME MUD AND I WILL PAINT THE SKIN OF VENUS".

EUGENE DELACROIX

INTRODUCTION

This family of earth colors complements the natural palette of neutrals. Terracotta, literally "fired earth," includes a variety of warm, rich colors from pale plaster pinkish red to deep earth red, with hot oranges somewhere in between. The basis for many of these colors are earth pigments, particularly those which are heated or roasted — burnt sienna and burnt umber, for example — to give deeper, more fiery shades.

These old colors, found inside and outside houses in practically every culture around the world, can be quite bright, although they lack the pure brilliance of primaries. Their softness and warmth make them easy to live with; the glow reflected from warm terracotta walls is exceptionally flattering, while the light in such rooms at all times of the day is beautifully golden, reminiscent of Mediterranean evenings.

Terracotta is emphatically not "peach." Peach, especially in its recent, more fashionable manifestations, can be remarkably insipid, the result of omitting the essential element of earthiness. Real terracotta suggests raw plaster, sun-dried earth, and warm sandstone.

136 TERRACOTTA

Because of these associations, it can often be effective to exaggerate the textural dimension. Paint can be applied in a bold wash or stippled to show patches of unevenness redolent of a rough, baked surface. This rather rustic effect is very compatible with the mellow shades of old polished wood.

Darker versions, tending toward a deep red-brown, work well with the refreshing contrast of blue or black and white. Blue and white crockery, black and white tiled floors, and checked or striped fabric all go well with a deep terracotta background. The look is not invariably countrified; the warm tones of any of these colors give an extra dimension of warmth and light in the city.

The clearest and least earthy of all the terracotta colors is orange, a color that is particularly associated with the wonderful checked fabrics of Madras. Orange, historically, was one of the fashionable shades of Art Deco, teamed with sharp lime green and cool blue. Orange and cool green make a fresh, invigorating combination.

THE WARMTH OF TERRACOTTA ON ROOF TILES AND ROUGH WALLS DISPLAYED IN A MEXICAN TERRACE.

CORAL

THIS WARMING, SUN-DRENCHED COLOR SCHEME FOR A BEDROOM IS BASED AROUND A PARTICULAR BURNT ORANGE SHADE, SLIGHTLY BRIGHTER THAN TRUE TERRACOTTA, MORE EARTHY THAN ORANGE. A WINDOW SHADE IN A DAPPLED PATTERN TINTS THE LIGHT, WHILE BED CURTAINS IN A WARM CHECK ADD TO THE MELLOW, GLOWING ATMOSPHERE. ANY ROOM WHICH FACES NORTH OR LACKS NATURAL LIGHT WOULD BENEFIT FROM SUCH ENRICHING COLORS. EVEN IF BED CURTAINS ARE NO LONGER A PRACTICAL NECESSITY IN CENTRALLY HEATED HOMES, THEY RETAIN THEIR DECORATIVE IMPACT, COUNTER-BALANCING THE EXPANSE OF THE BED AND OFFERING THE OPPORTUNITY FOR INJECTING LIVELY AREAS OF COLOR INTO A ROOM.

BRICK AND BLACK

TERRACOTTA COLORS
PRODUCE THE MOST
FLATTERING BACKGROUND,
EITHER PAINTED ON THE
WALLS TO REFLECT LIGHT OR
HUNG AT THE WINDOWS
FOR LIGHT TO FILTER
THROUGH. THESE WARM-
TO-HOT COLORS WORK
WELL WITH COLORS OF A
SIMILAR STRENGTH AND
INTENSITY – A VIVID STREAK
OF LIME, FOR EXAMPLE,
AND, OF COURSE, BLACK.
AT THE WINDOW, HOT
TERRACOTTA AND BUFF
STRIPED UNDERCURTAINS
HAVE FACING CURTAINS IN
A BOLD FRUIT PRINT. THE
CHAIRS ARE IN RICH
CONTRASTING PRINTS:
BLACK AND LIME SELF-
STRIPE, ALL COMPLEMENTED
BY A CLASSIC BLACK-AND-
WHITE MARBLE FLOOR.

SPICE

"SPICE" COLORS FORM AN IMPORTANT PART OF THE TERRACOTTA COLOR SPECTRUM. HERE, A PANELED ROOM IS THE SETTING FOR A MIXTURE OF BRIGHT YELLOW, DEEP RED, AND SAFFRON AND NUTMEG-BROWN, ALL DISPLAYED ON THE UPHOLSTERY OF SOFAS AND A COVERED STOOL. A ROOM MAY HAVE NEUTRAL-TONED WALLS AND FLOOR AND LITTLE IN THE WAY OF WINDOW TREATMENT YET STILL RETAIN A STRONG COLOR CHARACTER. THIS CAN BE ACHIEVED THROUGH THE JUDICIOUS USE OF FURNISHING FABRICS, IN THE FORM OF UPHOLSTERY OR FITTED COVERS.

FALL

THE TERRACOTTA PALETTE EMCOMPASSES THE FALL
VARIETY OF COLORS, FROM SHARP ORANGE TO RUSSET
AND EGG PLANT. THE STRONG EARTH COLORS
DISPLAYED ON MEDIEVAL ENCAUSTIC FLOORS, RIPE
FRUIT AND HARVEST VEGETABLES SUCH AS SQUASH
AND PUMPKINS, A BEECH WOODS WHEN THE LEAVES
HAVE TURNED, THE CORALS AND BLUSH ORANGES OF
SEASHELLS ARE STRIKING COLOR INSPIRATIONS. IN THE
INTERIOR, TERRACOTTA NATURALLY COMES IN THE
FORM OF TILED FLOORS AND WARM WOOD TONES;
LIGHTER VERSIONS OF THE COLOR IN THE APPEALING
COLOR OF RAW PLASTER, CHARMINGLY UNEVEN AND
WARM IN TONE. SUCH COLORS ARE VERY CLOSE TO THE
POMPEIIAN RED WHICH SO ENTRANCED THE
ARCHITECTS AND DESIGNERS OF THE
NINETEENTH-CENTURY NEOCLASSICAL PERIOD.

MADRAS

AN EASY WAY TO DRESS A BED IS TO THROW A LENGTH OF CLOTH OVER A SIMPLE ARMATURE AND ALLOW IT TO DRAPE TO THE SIDES. THE DEEP SHELL PINK AND TERRACOTTA COLORS OF THIS COMBINATION RECALL THE WONDERFUL MIXTURES IN TRADITIONAL MADRAS PATTERNS: CLEAR ORANGE, PINK, YELLOW, AND GREEN IN SUBTLE CHECKS AND STRIPES. THE KELIM CARPET DISPLAYS ALL THE COLORS IN THE ROOM, ANCHORING THE SCHEME. A FAVORITE RUG OR A PAINTING CAN BE A FRUITFUL STARTING POINT FOR DECORATIVE IDEAS.

148 TERRACOTTA

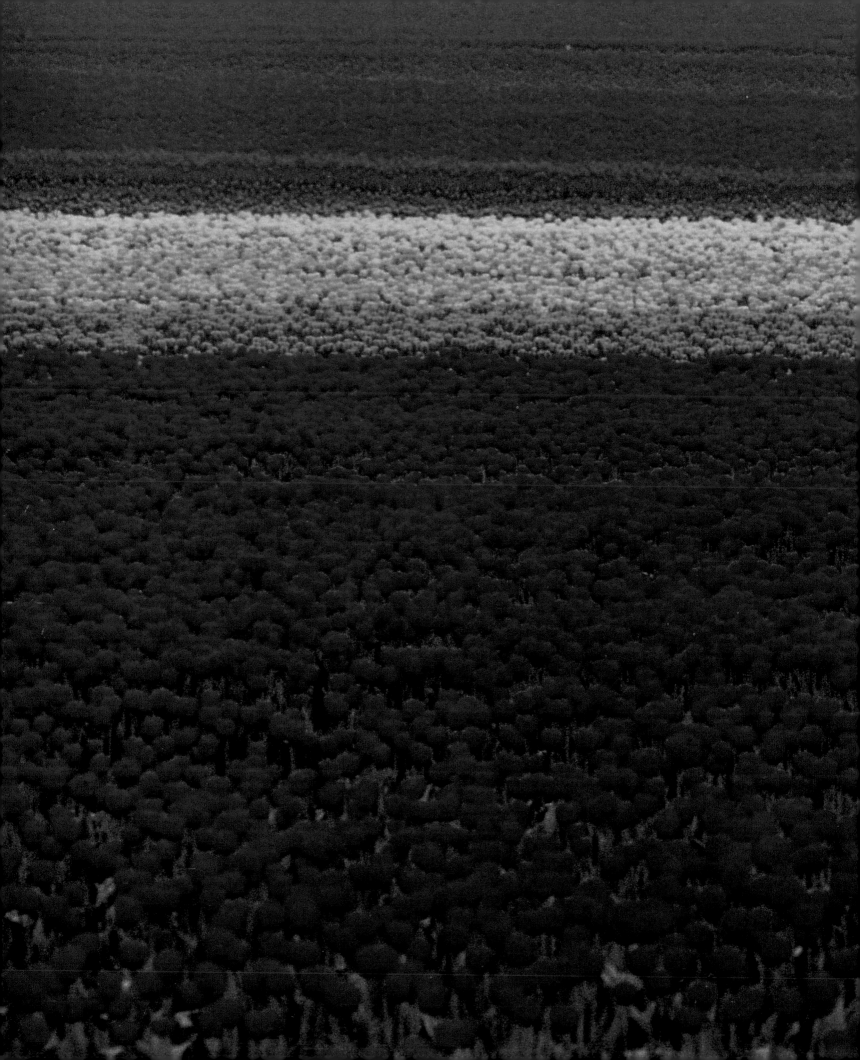

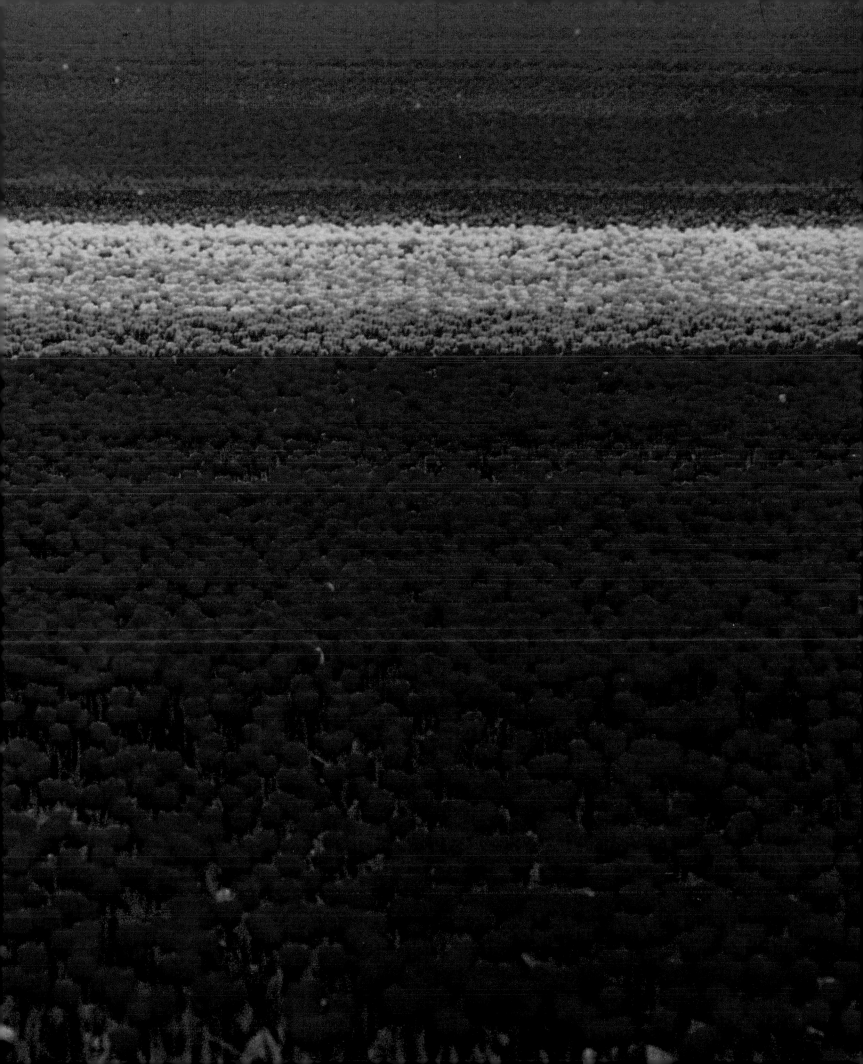

R E D

"A FIERCE VINDICTIVE SCRIBBLE OF RED".

INTRODUCTION

Red arouses. Hot, passionate, rich and celebratory, red is a siren shade, a color to revel in. The Chinese color of luck and happiness, the marriage color of India, red is the color of love and romance, of courage, passion, and rage. Red means danger, stop, fire; in nature, red is the accent that signals the poisonous berries, the ripe fruit, or the bright courtship display. It is a uniquely assertive and vigorous color.

In decoration red has always signified richness and luxury. This basic association is hardly surprising, since pigments and dyes giving bright vivid reds were expensive and rare until the new synthetic colors of the mid-nineteenth century were introduced. Early in the history of interior design, red silk damask stretched over the walls was the height of sophisticated display and made a sumptuous glowing background in glittering state rooms. Red was believed to be the best foil for paintings; as well as in picture galleries, red walls often featured in dining rooms or grand rooms otherwise used for entertaining, where the intention was to generate excitement and show off wealth.

Today many people are wary of using red in large quantities, just as they hesitate before using any strong, saturated color. But to rule out the possibilities of decorating with red, or basing a color scheme around it, is to miss the warmth and vitality that previous generations understood and heartily appreciated. Even quite small rooms can look wonderful in red, lending them a jewel-like intensity.

Red is a natural accent and for those who are incurably shy of making a bold statement, this may be the best way of learning to enjoy the color. A red quilt, a splash of red in a tablecloth or as part of the sofa upholstery draws any room together successfully.

Pink is not light red, but a color in its own right. Where red is bold and brave, pink is delicate and soothing, a flattering, warm color in all its manifestations from the lightest rose pink to shocking Schiaparelli. Very blue or cool pinks can sometimes look pasty, but in its subtle form pink is unbeatably refined and beautifully luxurious.

EIGHTEENTH-CENTURY PANELING PAINTED *SANG DE BOEUF* IS EVOCATIVE OF ANOTHER AGE.

WINTER RED

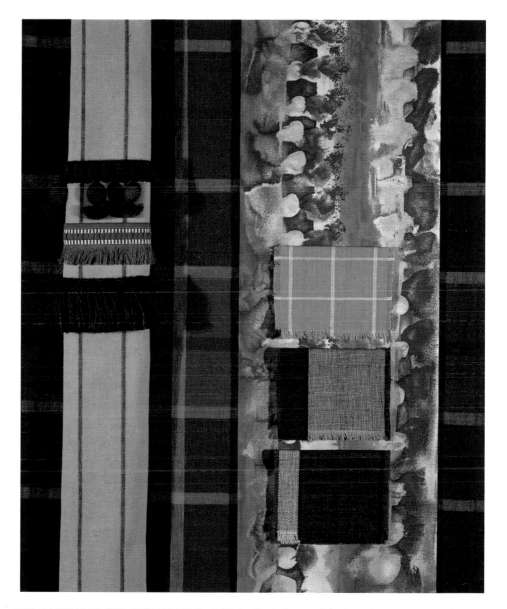

EYE-CATCHING CRIMSON IS WARMING AND LIVELY, A COLOR TO CHEER UP COLD, GRAY WINTER DAYS. THIS EXUBERANTLY DRESSED BED, WITH ITS FLASH OF RED QUILT AND SIMPLE HANGINGS, WOULD BANISH THE CHILL. RED HAS ALWAYS FEATURED IN TRADITIONAL PATTERNS SUCH AS PLAID TARTANS, WHERE IT IS TYPICALLY COMBINED WITH DEEP FIR GREEN AND A RICH, WARM YELLOW. A REALLY VIVID CLEAR RED SUCH AS CRIMSON IS AN EXCITING AND DEMANDING COLOR. INTRODUCE LIMITED AREAS OF BRIGHT RED IN THE FORM OF A QUILT, TABLECLOTH, LAMPSHADE, PAINTED DOOR, OR THROW: EVEN IN SMALL DOSES, ITS ABILITY TO ADD VITALITY TO A ROOM IS SECOND TO NONE.

RED 159

RED AND WHITE

WHITE DOMESTICATES RED, JUST AS IT ADDS A HOMEY QUALITY TO BLUES AND GREENS. RED-AND-WHITE CHECKED GINGHAM IS ALMOST SYNONYMOUS WITH HOSPITALITY; RED CHECKS, CALICO, OR STRIPED FABRICS ARE COMMON IN EVERYDAY USE THROUGHOUT EUROPE AND AMERICA. THE FRESHNESS AND GAIETY OF RED AND WHITE MAKE AN IRRESISTIBLE COMBINATION, AS DISPLAYED BY THE RED PAINTED CASEMENT WINDOW IN THIS IRISH COTTAGE, FRAMING ROWS OF DAINTY LACE PANELS (LEFT). SOME RED AND WHITE COMBINATIONS ARE INHERENTLY MORE ELEGANT AND REFINED, SUCH AS THE CLASSIC *TOILE DE JOUY* PATTERN IN SOFT MADDER RED, A HINT OF WHICH IS SEEN IN THE DESIGN OF THIS PLATE (RIGHT).

EASTERN RED

CRIMSON AND GOLD CURTAINS GENERATE A MOOD OF ORIENTAL RICHNESS COMBINED WITH A FACING DRAPERY IN SWIRLING BURGUNDY PAISLEY. THE VICTORIANS WERE PARTICULARLY FOND OF STRONG, ENVELOPING REDS AND USED THEM TO GREAT EFFECT IN THEIR LAVISHLY FURNISHED ROOMS. ALL REDS LOOK WONDERFUL BY SOFT CANDLELIGHT OR FIRELIGHT, AND SUIT ROOMS THAT ARE USED FOR ENTERTAINING AND DINING. STRONG TO DEEP REDS OCCUR IN MANY EASTERN AND NEAR-EASTERN TEXTILES, IN KELIMS, CARPETS, PAISLEY FABRICS, AND INTRICATELY EMBROIDERED HANGINGS. LAYERS OF THESE PATTERNS CAN BE BUILT UP EASILY AND NATURALLY, EACH COMPLEMENTING AND ECHOING THE OTHERS. AS IN ORIENTAL DESIGNS, BLUE-GREEN IS A GOOD PARTNER, BUT THE LIVELIEST ACCENT IS GOLD. TOUCHES OF GLITTER, IN A ROPE TIE-BACK, FRINGE, OR AS HERE, IN THE BOLD, STRIPED FABRIC ON A FOOTSTOOL, CATCH THE LIGHT AND ADD A RICH, GLOWING ATMOSPHERE.

ELECTRIC RED

RED IS THE COLOR IN THE SPECTRUM WHICH DRAWS THE
EYE THE MOST. SENSATIONAL EFFECTS CAN BE CREATED
BY SETTING RED WITH ITS COMPLEMENTARY OR
OPPOSITE AND REVELING IN THE RESULTING
DYNAMISM. RED AND GREEN IN VARIOUS
COMBINATIONS VIBRATE; RED AND STRONG BLUE CAN
ALSO GENERATE GREAT COLOR EXCITEMENT. MONET
DELIBERATELY JUXTAPOSED COMPLEMENTARIES: RED
POPPIES IN A GREEN FIELD. BRIGHT COLOR HAS A
PRIMITIVE POWER AND ENERGY; IT IS THERE IN NATURE,
IN FLOWERS, LEAVES, AND SEEDPODS, AND IT IS PART
OF EVERY CULTURE. EVEN IF YOU DO NOT DECORATE
YOUR ENTIRE HOME IN BRILLIANT SHADES, YOU CAN
BRING A CORNER TO LIFE BY ASSEMBLING A COLOR
DISPLAY. A BOWL OF FRUIT, A VASE OF FLOWERS, A
COLLECTION OF PLATES, THE INGREDIENTS COULD NOT
BE SIMPLER OR MORE ACCESSIBLE.

RICH RED

RED FOR LUXURY OR RICHNESS IS A TRADITIONAL ASSOCIATION, DATING FROM THE TIME WHEN RED SILK DAMASK WAS THE HEIGHT OF FURNISHING FASHION. YOU CAN BORROW AN ELEMENT OF THIS GRANDEUR BY ADDING RUBY-RED DETAILS SUCH AS PILLOWS AND THROWS IN FINE FABRICS LIKE SATIN AND SILK (ABOVE LEFT AND RIGHT). PILLOW COVERS ARE AN IDEAL WAY OF INTRODUCING COLOR NOTES TO BRIGHTEN OR ENRICH A ROOM. AND BECAUSE THE AMOUNT OF FABRIC REQUIRED IS LIMITED, YOU CAN AFFORD TO BE MORE EXTRAVAGANT IN TERMS OF MATERIAL AND TRIMMING. THE WARM, RICH REDS WORK WELL WITH BUTTERCUP YELLOWS AND GOLD (RIGHT).

PINK

PINK CAN BE AS PLAIN AS A PLASTERED WALL OR COLORWASHED STUCCO, A ROBUST SHADE FOUND ON THE OUTSIDE OF HOUSES FROM TUSCANY TO PROVENCE TO SUFFOLK, ENGLAND (LEFT). PRETTY, DELICATE, AND LUXURIOUS, PINK HAS ANOTHER MOOD, FOREVER ASSOCIATED WITH THE ROCOCO FANCIES OF MADAME DE POMPADOUR. STRAWBERRY SATIN, SHELL-STRIPED BROCADES, AND FLORAL COTTONS ARE IRRESISTIBLE. FLATTERING, WARM, AND ELEGANT, THIS IS THE CLASSIC COLOR FOR A TRADITIONALLY FEMININE BEDROOM.

168 RED

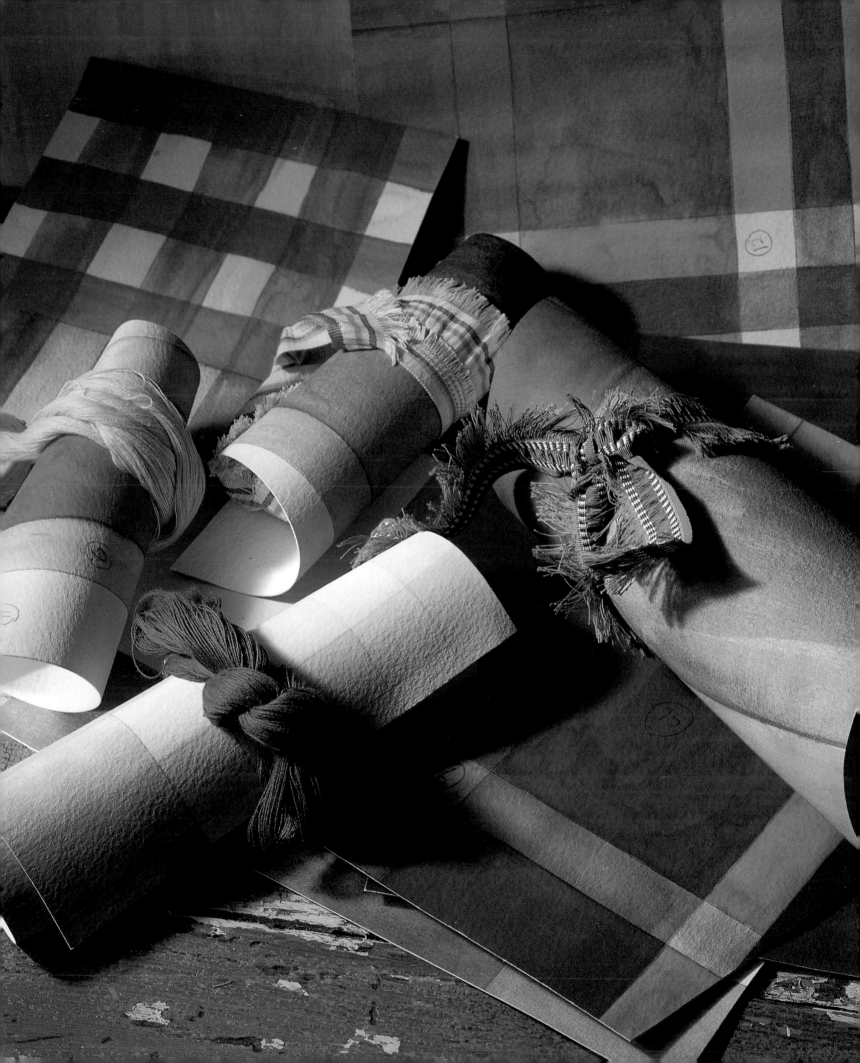

COLOR PALETTES

"THIS TIME IT'S JUST SIMPLY MY BEDROOM, ONLY HERE COLOR IS TO DO EVERYTHING, AND GIVING BY ITS SIMPLIFICATION A GRANDER STYLE TO THINGS, IS TO BE SUGGESTIVE HERE OF *REST* OR OF SLEEP IN GENERAL. IN A WORD, TO LOOK AT THE PICTURE OUGHT TO REST THE BRAIN OR RATHER THE IMAGINATION.
THE WALLS ARE PALE VIOLET. THE FLOOR IS OF RED TILES. THE WOOD OF THE BED AND CHAIRS IS THE YELLOW OF FRESH BUTTER, THE SHEET AND PILLOWS VERY LIGHT LEMON-GREEN.
THE COVERLET SCARLET. THE WINDOW GREEN.
THE TOILET TABLE ORANGE, THE BASIN BLUE.
THE DOORS LILAC.
AND THAT IS ALL – THERE IS NOTHING IN THIS ROOM WITH CLOSED SHUTTERS".

LETTER TO HIS BROTHER THEO,
VINCENT VAN GOGH

COLOR PALETTES

THE FOLLOWING PAGES COMPRISE SEVEN DISTINCT COLOR PALETTES BASED ON THE MAIN SECTIONS OF THE BOOK: WHITE, BLUE, GREEN, YELLOW, NATURAL, TERRACOTTA, AND RED. EACH OFFERS A COLOR FAMILY IN FABRIC AND WALLPAPERS SO YOU CAN SEE THE FULL RANGE AT A GLANCE AND DECIDE ON YOUR OWN PREFERENCES. IN ADDITION, FOUR COLOR

SAMPLES HAVE BEEN CHOSEN WHICH REPRESENT COMPATIBLE OR COMPLEMENTARY SHADES TO EACH MAIN COLOR, GIVING INSPIRATION FOR A WIDER COLOR PALETTE. THE ILLUSTRATION BELOW IS A KEY TO IDENTIFYING THE FABRIC AND WALLPAPER NAMES AND COLORS THAT APPEAR IN THE PALETTES ON PAGES 173-185.

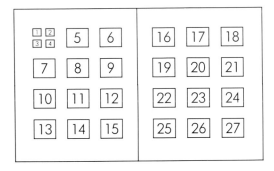

WHITE COLOR PALETTE

1 DOUBLEGLAZE F38/15
2 FIREFLY F272/03
3 DOUBLEGLAZE F38/02
4 FIREFLY F272/53
5 FIREFLY F272/30
6 BANOL F180/05
7 SEDGE F261/08
8 MARQUETRY F258/01
9 KASAN F232/05
10 DAMAS FLEURI F131/08
11 RUSH F260/07
12 TIMUR F245/01
13 CASSIS F182/05
14 SIRSI F317/02
15 MANOSQUE F184/06

11 CASSIA F130/12
12 MANOSQUE F184/01
13 RUSH F260/08
14 MIREPOIX F183/01
15 SEDGE F261/09
16 BAKU P159/07
17 COLONNA P173/10
18 VIOTTOLO P174/08
19 STUCCO STRIPE P133/08
20 BAKU P159/27
21 PASSAGGIO P135/02
22 DOUBLEGLAZE F38/27
23 TANDA F321/01
24 THIZY F246/04
25 DEJEUNER SUR L'HERBE F251/01
26 DOUBLEGLAZE F38/28
27 AMBALA F318/03

BLUE COLOR PALETTE

1 DOUBLEGLAZE F38/11
2 DOUBLEGLAZE F38/13
3 FIREFLY F272/59
4 SIRSI F317/09
5 TWINKLE TWINKLE P162/06
6 BAKU P159/06
7 CANDY STRIPE P140/02
8 STUCCO P10/21
9 STUCCO P10/22
10 DOUBLEGLAZE F38/26

GREEN COLOR PALETTE

1 FIREFLY F272/67
2 FIREFLY F272/48
3 FIREFLY F272/53
4 DOUBLEGLAZE F38/41
5 DIAMANTE P136/05
6 STUCCO P10/10
7 MIANE P148/07
8 BAKU P159/01
9 PAGLIA P11/04

10 NANTUA F287/16
11 BIHAR F322/04
12 DOUBLEGLAZE F38/33
13 SEDGE F261/11
14 DOUBLEGLAZE F38/32
15 MARQUETRY F259/33
16 MIRANDOLA P146/03
17 PASSAGGIO P135/01
18 BAKU P159/05
19 SOLFERINO P145/09
20 MONTEBULLUNA P147/08
21 STUCCO P10/09
22 KASHGAR F233/05
23 SIRSI F317/08
24 DOUBLEGLAZE F38/30
25 RUSH F260/11
26 MANOSQUE F184/03
27 SEDGE F261/12

YELLOW COLOR PALETTE

1 DOUBLEGLAZE F38/13
2 DOUBLEGLAZE F38/05
3 DOUBLEGLAZE F38/27
4 DOUBLEGLAZE F38/12
5 CANDY STRIPE P140/04
6 SOLFERINO P145/05
7 DOTTY P141/04
8 STUCCO P10/18
9 BAKU P159/15
10 FIREFLY F272/28
11 DOUBLEGLAZE F30/35
12 LAPALME F185/04
13 RUSH F260/06
14 FIREFLY F272/03
15 SEDGE F261/05
16 STUCCO F10/07
17 TWINKLE TWINKLE P162/03
18 STUCCO P10/18
19 TWINKLE TWINKLE P162/07
20 BAKU P159/13
21 PASSAGGIO P135/03
22 MIREPOIX F183/04
23 KASHGAR F233/01
24 LAPALISSE F286/10
25 NANTUA F287/17
26 DOUBLEGLAZE F38/39
27 RUSH F260/04

NATURAL COLOR PALETTE

1 DOUBLEGLAZE F38/34
2 DOUBLEGLAZE F38/19
3 DOUBLEGLAZE F38/38
4 FIREFLY F272/18
5 PASSAGGIO P135/07
6 CASPIAN ROSE P154/05
7 BAKU P159/08
8 VIOTTOLO P174/04
9 HICKETY PICKETY P161/02
10 LICHEN P226/02
11 SEDGE F261/06
12 FIREFLY F272/36
13 SEDGE F261/07
14 LAPALISSE F286/03
15 MARQUETRY F258/12
16 TWINKLE TWINKLE P162/08
17 SOLFERINO P145/06
18 STUCCO P10/05

19 BAKU P159/10
20 MIRANDOLA P146/05
21 TAORMINA P150/21
22 FIREFLY F272/21
23 SEDGE F261/04
24 RUSH F260/13
25 THIZY F246/08
26 FIREFLY F272/24
27 TANDA F321/03

TERRACOTTA COLOR PALETTE

1 DOUBLEGLAZE F38/41
2 FIREFLY F272/59
3 DOUBLEGLAZE F38/36
4 FIREFLY F272/07
5 DOTTY P141/03
6 BAKU P159/19
7 TWINKLE TWINKLE P162/05
8 LEAF FRESCO P13/06
9 BAKU P159/21
10 FIREFLY F272/13
11 SEDGE F261/03
12 DAMAS FLEURI F131/04
13 MANOSQUE F184/04
14 DOUBLEGLAZE F38/17
15 KASHGAR F233/04
16 STUCCO P10/17
17 STUCCO STRIPE P133/02
18 STUCCO P10/03
19 ASTRAKHAN P152/05
20 VIOTTOLO P174/07
21 PASSAGGIO P135/04
22 FIREFLY P272/19
23 LAPALISSE F286/06
24 SIRSI F317/04
25 LAPALME F185/03
26 OOTY F320/01
27 FIREFLY F272/17

RED COLOR PALETTE

1 FIREFLY F272/30
2 DOUBLEGLAZE F38/27
3 FIREFLY F272/41
4 FIREFLY F272/01
5 FILIGRANA P138/01
6 CANDY STRIPE P140/06
7 TWINKLE TWINKLE P162/04
8 BAKU P159/22
9 DUSHAK P153/06
10 CROSSPATCH F194/07
11 FIREFLY F272/05
12 MARQUETRY F258/41
13 FIREFLY F272/06
14 MONTFERRAT F179/01
15 DOUBLEGLAZE F38/21
16 MONTEBULLUNA P147/04
17 ASTRAKHAN P152/07
18 STUCCO P010/04
19 STUCCO STRIPE P133/01
20 CARIOLA P015/01
21 PASSAGGIO P135/06
22 MIREPOIX F183/05
23 FIREFLY F272/07
24 ORISSA F314/03
25 LAPALISSE F286/05
26 THIZY F246/01
27 RUSH F260/02

WHITE COLOR PALETTE

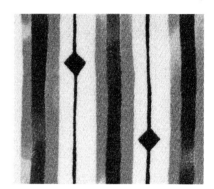

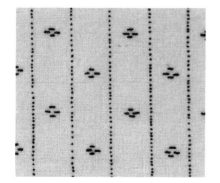

BLUE COLOR PALETTE

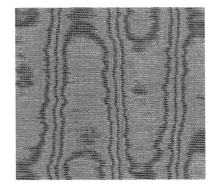
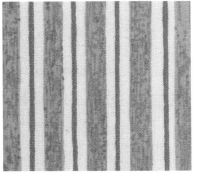

BLUE 175

GREEN COLOR PALETTE

 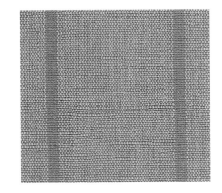 

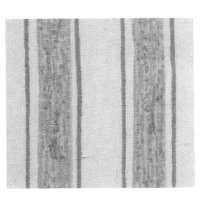  

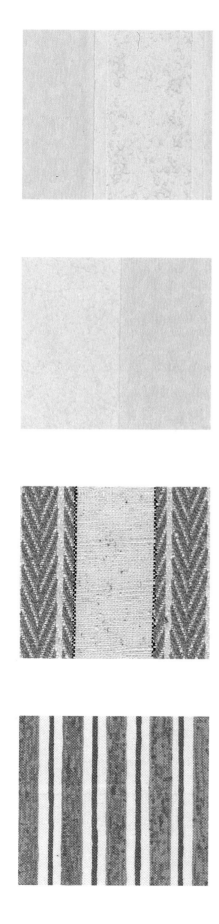
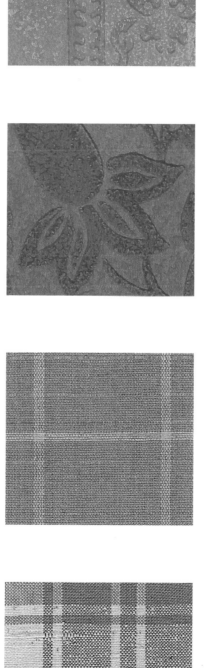

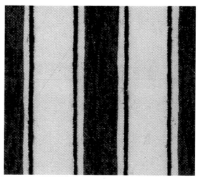

GREEN 177

YELLOW 179

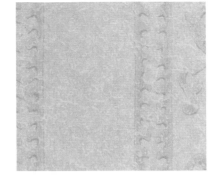

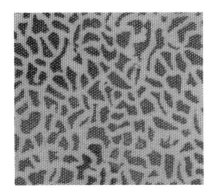
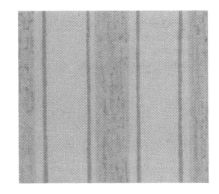

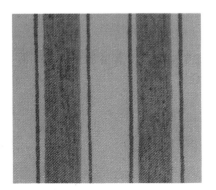

TERRACOTTA COLOR PALETTE

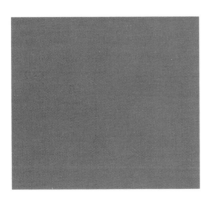

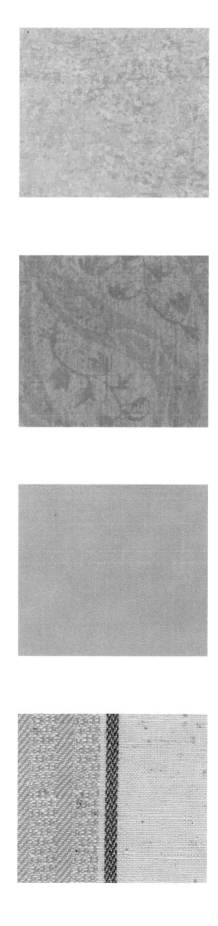

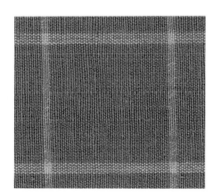

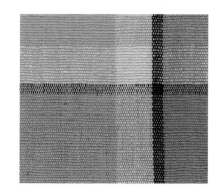

TERRACOTTA 183

RED COLOR PALETTE

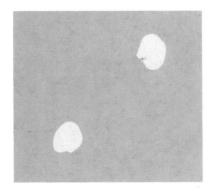  

 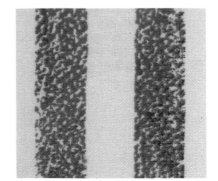 

RED 185

FABRIC DIRECTORY

EACH OF THE FOLLOWING ILLUSTRATIONS IDENTIFIES THE DESIGNERS GUILD FABRICS FEATURED IN THE ROOM SETS THROUGHOUT THE BOOK.

WHITE LIGHT page 40

1 NANTUA F287/01
2 SEERSUCKER T11/07
3 DAMAS FLEURI F131/08
4 HOPSACK F330/01
5 DOUBLEGLAZE F38/01

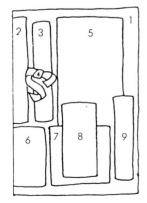

CLASSICAL STRIPE page 45

1 SIRSI F317/06
2 THIZY F246/07
3 SEDGE F261/08
4 OCONA T23/03
5 PROVENCE F174/02
6 LA VERDIERE F176/02
7 MANOSQUE F184/06
8 LAPALME F185/06
9 CASTELLANE F186/05

FRENCH BLUE page 54

1 VIOTTOLO P174/08
2 CHIMU T8/05
3 SEERSUCKER T11/05
4 TUFTS T13/05
5 RIVOLO F274/02
6 PUNTASPILLE F275/02
7 THIZY F246/04
8 PERGAMENA F276/03

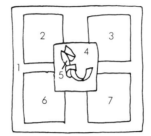

CHECKS AND SPOTS page 59

1 CASTELLANE F186/01
2 JALNA F325/07
3 MIREPOIX F183/02
4 SIRSI F317/03
5 BIHAR F322/05
6 BANDRA F324/01
7 MANOSQUE F184/01
8 LA VERDIERE F176/01
9 SEDGE F261/09

ITALIAN CHECK page 65

1 COCHIN F316/04
2 AMBALA F318/03
3 MYSORE F315/05
4 SIRSI F317/05
5 OCONA T23/01
6 SIRSI F317/10
7 TANDA F321/01

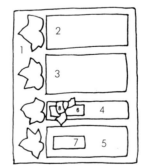

PISTACHIO page 80

1 BAKU P159/01
2 ORISSA F314/01
3 ARANI F319/04
4 BIHAR F322/04
5 SIRSI F317/08
6 MANOSQUE F184/06
7 SIRSI F317/09
8 OCONA F323/03

GARDEN page 84

1 SIRSI F317/08
2 THE MELON PATCH F312/03
3 OOTY F320/03
4 ORISSA F314/05
5 ORISSA F314/04
6 OCONA T23/02
7 HARVEST F313/04
8 MYSORE F315/04
9 OCONA T23/06

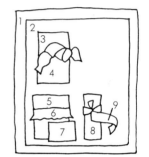

APPLE GREEN page 88

1 COLONNA P173/06
2 KASAN F232/03
3 CHAZELLE F240/01
4 NELL O'RTO P175/01
5 GHIRLANDA F280/01
6 NANTUA F287/16
7 PASSARIANO F204/05
8 OCONA T23/03

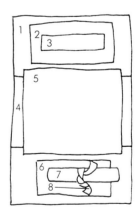

CHROME YELLOW page 102

1 NANTUA F287/18
2 NANTUA F287/15
3 NANTUA F287/04
4 TUFTS T19/02
5 ORION T18/02
6 HUARI T22/05
7 HUARI T22/04

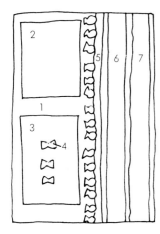

GOLD page 106

1 CHIMU T08/03
2 CHAZELLE F240/03
3 NELL O'RTO F279/02
4 ASIAGO F205/01
5 NANTUA F287/17
6 GIVORS F239/01
7 THIZY F246/05

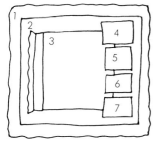

TUSCAN GLOW page 114
For diagram, see CHECKS
AND SPOTS, opposite.

1 JALNA F325/05
2 OOTY F320/02
3 JALNA F325/02
4 VITA F323/01
5 SUKMA F326/01
6 TANDA F321/02
7 COCHIN F316/02
8 BANDRA F324/02
9 JALNA F325/06

DRIFTWOOD page 127

1 SIRSI F317/01
2 COCHIN F316/03
3 TRACER F294/03
4 LEAFLIGHT F295/03
5 ARIANI F319/03
6 TANDA F321/03
7 CHIMU T08/07
8 TUFT T13/07

FRESCO page 130

1 TORCELLO P150/01
2 MIRANDOLA P146/02
3 SOLFERINO P145/01
4 BAKU P159/09
5 STUCCO P10/15
6 MANDRIA P151/02
7 CARIOLA P15/07

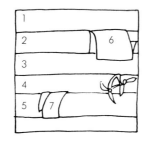

CORAL page 140

1 STUCCO P10/03
2 COCHIN F316/01
3 CHIMU T08/02
4 DOUBLEGLAZE F38/01
5 CORAL T10/02
6 SIRSI F317/06
7 SIRSI F317/04
8 ORISSA F314/02
9 BIHAR F322/04

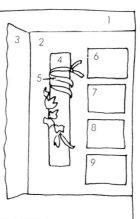

SPICE page 144
From top to bottom:

1 NANTUA F287/19
2 MYSORE F315/03
3 LAPALISSE F286/06
4 ARANI F319/02

MADRAS page 148

1 OOTY F320/01
2 HARVEST F313/01
3 SEERSUCKER T11/02
4 THE MELON PATCH F312/01
5 AURICULA F288/01
6 BIHAR F322/06
7 ONION T8/04

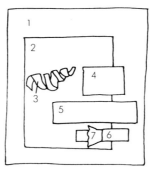

WINTER RED page 159

1 ORISSA F314/03
2 RUCHE T16/04
3 BIHAR F322/01
4 SIRSI F317/08
5 AMBALA F318/01
6 AMBALA F318/02
7 ONION T18/04
8 OCONA T23/01

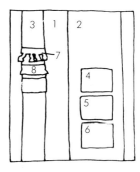

EASTERN RED page 163

1 TIMUR F245/04
2 FAN EDGE T4/04
3 THIZY F246/01
4 ASTRAKHAN F242/05
5 FAN EDGE T4/04
6 BOKHARA F244/05
7 TUMBEZ T3/05

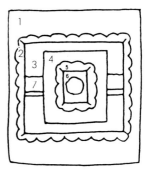

DESIGNERS GUILD DISTRIBUTORS

Designers Guild fabrics and wallpapers are distributed in America through the following agents:

ATLANTA
AINSWORTH NOAH AND ASSOCIATES INC, 351 Peachtree Hills Avenue – Suite 518, Atlanta, Georgia 30305. Tel: 404 231 8787

BOSTON
SHECTER MARTIN, One Design Center Place – Suite 111, Boston, Massachusetts 02210. Tel: 617 951 2526

OSBORNE AND LITTLE
Merchandise Mart – Suite 610 Chicago, Illinois, 60654. Tel: 312 467 0913

DALLAS
BOYD LEVINSON & COMPANY, 1400-C HiLine Drive, Dallas, Texas 75207. Tel: 214 698 0226

DANIA
DESIGN WEST INC – DCOTA, 1855 Griffin Road – Suite A474, Dania, Florida 33004. Tel: 954 925 8225

DENVER
SHANAHAN COLLECTION, Denver Design Centre, 595 S. Broadway, Suite 100-S, Denver, Colorado 80209. Tel: 303 778 7088

HOUSTON
BOYD LEVINSON & COMPANY, 5120 Woodway – Suite 4001, Houston, Texas 77056. Tel: 713 623 2344

LOS ANGELES
OAKMONT, Pacific Design Centre, Suite B647, 8687 Melrose Avenue, Los Angeles, California 90069. Tel: 310 659 1423

MINNEAPOLIS
GENE SMILEY SHOWROOM, International Market, Square, 275 Market Street, Suite 321, Minneapolis, Minnesota 55405. Tel: 612 332 0402

NEW JERSEY
DAVID PARRET, 14 East Lane, Madison 07940. Tel: 201 635 5545

NEW YORK
OSBORNE & LITTLE, 979 Third Avenue – Suite 520, New York, New York 10022. Tel: 212 751 3333

PHILADELPHIA
JW SHOWROOM, INC., The Marketplace – Suite 304, 2400 Market Street, Philadelphia, Pennsylvania, 19103. Tel: 215 561 2270

PORTLAND
STEPHEN E. EARLS SHOWROOMS, 208 NW 21st Avenue – Suite 200, Portland, Oregon 97209. Tel: 503 227 0541

SAN FRANCISCO
RANDOLPH & HEIN INC., Galleria Design Center – Suite 101, 101 Henry Adams Street, San Francisco, California 94103. Tel: 415 864 3550

SCOTTSDALE SWILLEY-FRANCOEUR & HUNTER, 2712 North 68th Street, Suite 4000, Scottsdale, Arizona 85257. Tel: 602 990 1745

SEATTLE
STEPHEN E EARLS SHOWROOMS, 520 South Findlay Street, Seattle, Washington 98108. Tel: 206 767 7220

STAMFORD
OSBORNE & LITTLE INC., 65 Commerce Road, Stamford, Connecticut 06902. Tel: 203 359 1500

WASHINGTON DC
OSBORNE & LITTLE, 300D Street SW – Suite 435, Washington DC 20024. Tel: 202 554 8800

CANADA
PRIMAVERA, 160 Pears Avenue – Suite 210, Toronto, M5R 1T2. Tel: 416 921 3334

ACKNOWLEDGMENTS

The publisher thanks the following photographers and organizations for their kind permission to reproduce the photographs in this book:
5 above center Dominic Sansoni/Impact Photos; 5 above right Carlos Navajas; 5 center left Carlos Navajas; 5 center Tim Woodcock/TWP; 5 below left Jean-Pierre Godeaut; 5 below center Ian A Griffiths/Robert Harding; 8-9 James Morris; 10 below left Patricia Aithie/Ffotograff; 17 Paul Forster/Impact Photos; 19 The Tate Gallery, London (courtesy of Howard Hodgkin); 27 below and center David Montgomery/Conran Octopus; 28 above Jean-Pierre Godeaut; 28 below Christian Sarramon; 29 Christopher Rennie/Robert Harding; 30 David Montgomery/Conran Octopus; 32-3 Carlos Navajas; 35 above left Carlos Navajas; 35 above right Patricia Aithie/Ffotograff; 35 below left Carlos Navajas; 35 below right Dominic Sansoni/Impact Photos; 38-9 Jean-Pierre Godeaut (Catherine Margaretis); 42 left Elizabeth Whiting and Associates/Cassell; 42 right La Maison de Marie Claire/Snitt/Bayle; 43 Elizabeth Whiting and Associates/Cassell; 46-7 Laurence Delderfield; 49 above left Christian Sarramon; 49 above right S & O Mathews; 49 below left Carlos Navajas; 49 below right Patricia Aithie/Ffotograff; 52-3 Guy Bouchet; 56 Elizabeth Whiting and Associates/Cassell; 57 Elizabeth Whiting and Associates/Cassell; 60 above Nedra Westwater/Robert Harding; 61 above right Peter Moszynski/The Hutchison Library; 61 below left Carlos Navajas; 62 right Robin Guild; 63 Christian Sarramon; 67 below left Laurence Delderfield; 68-9 Carlos Navajas; 71 above left Richard Bryant/Arcaid (courtesy of the Mount Vernon Ladies Association); 71 above right Robin Guild; 71 below left David Montgomery/Conran Octopus; 72-3 Schuster/Robert Harding; 75 above left Carlos Navajas; 75 below left Mark Cator/Impact Photos; 75 below right Jacqui Hurst; 78-9 La Maison de Marie Claire/Bailache/Rozensztroch; 86 Mike England; 87 Christian Sarramon; 92 below Laurence Delderfield; 93 Guy Bouchet; 94-5 Steve Bavister/Robert Harding; 97 above left Ken Gillham/Robert Harding; 97 above right Tim Woodcock/TWP; 97 below left Philippe Perdereau; 97 below right Christian Sarramon; 101 Guy Bouchet; 104 Jacqui Hurst; 105 Michael Boys/Boys Syndication; 109 Richard Bryant/Arcaid (Homewood House); 110 Christian Sarramon; 112 below Guy Bouchet; 112-3 above Steven Moore/Impact Photos; 116 Dominic Sansoni/Impact Photos; 117 Tim Woodcock/TWP; 118-9 Martin Black/Impact Photos; 121 above left Jacqui Hurst; 121 above right Peter Ryan/Robert Harding; 121 below left Carlos Navajas; 125 Jean-Pierre Godeaut; 128 above Carlos Navajas; 129 above right Tim Woodcock/TWP; 129 below left Walter Rawlings/Robert Harding; 135 above left Jean-Pierre Godeaut; 135 above right Christian Sarramon; 135 below left Robin Guild; 135 below right Liba Taylor/The Hutchison Library; 138-9 La Maison de Marie Claire/Beaufre/Billaud; 146 below Jean-Pierre Godeaut; 147 above left Guy Bouchet; 150-1 Robert Dowling/Robert Harding; 153 above left Ian A Griffiths/Robert Harding; 153 above right Tim Woodcock/TWP; 153 below left Tim Woodcock/TWP; 153 below right Jacqui Hurst; 156-7 The World of Interiors/Tim Beddow; 160 Robert Francis/The Hutchison Library; 164 above S & O Mathews; 165 above right Jesco Von Puttkamer/The Hutchison Library; 165 below left Christian Sarramon; 168 Christian Sarramon.

The following photographs were specially taken by David Montgomery for Designers Guild: 1-4, 5 above left, 6, 10 above and center, 10 below right, 12-3, 14, 15, 16, 20, 21, 23, 26, 27 above, 31, 36-7, 41, 44, 50-1, 55, 58, 60 below, 61 above left, 61 below right, 62 left, 64-5, 66, 67 above, 67 below left, 70, 71 below right, 76-7, 80-1, 82-5, 89, 90, 91, 92 above, 98-9, 103, 107, 108, 111, 112 above, 112-3 below, 113, 114, 122-3, 126, 128 below, 129 above left, 129 below right, 130-1, 132-3, 136-7, 141, 142-3, 144-5, 146 above, 147 above right, 147 below, 149, 154-5, 158-9, 161, 162, 164 below, 165 above left, 165 below right, 166-7, 169, 170, 189, 192.

The publisher would like to thank Harper Collins Publishers for their kind permission to reproduce extracts from *The Letters of Vincent Van Gogh* on pages 11, 118 and 171.

INDEX